World Wisdom

The Library of Perennial Philosophy

The Library of Perennial Philosophy is dedicated to the exposition of the timeless Truth underlying the diverse religions. This Truth, often referred to as the *Sophia Perennis*—or Perennial Wisdom—finds its expression in the revealed Scriptures as well as the writings of the great sages and the artistic creations of the traditional worlds.

An Illustrated Introduction to Taoism: The Wisdom of the Sages appears as one of our selections in the Treasures of the World's Religions series.

Treasures of the World's Religions Series

This series of anthologies presents scriptures and the writings of the great spiritual authorities of the past on fundamental themes. Some titles are devoted to a single spiritual tradition, while others have a unifying topic that touches upon traditions from both the East and West, such as prayer and virtue. Some titles have a companion volume within the Perennial Philosophy series.

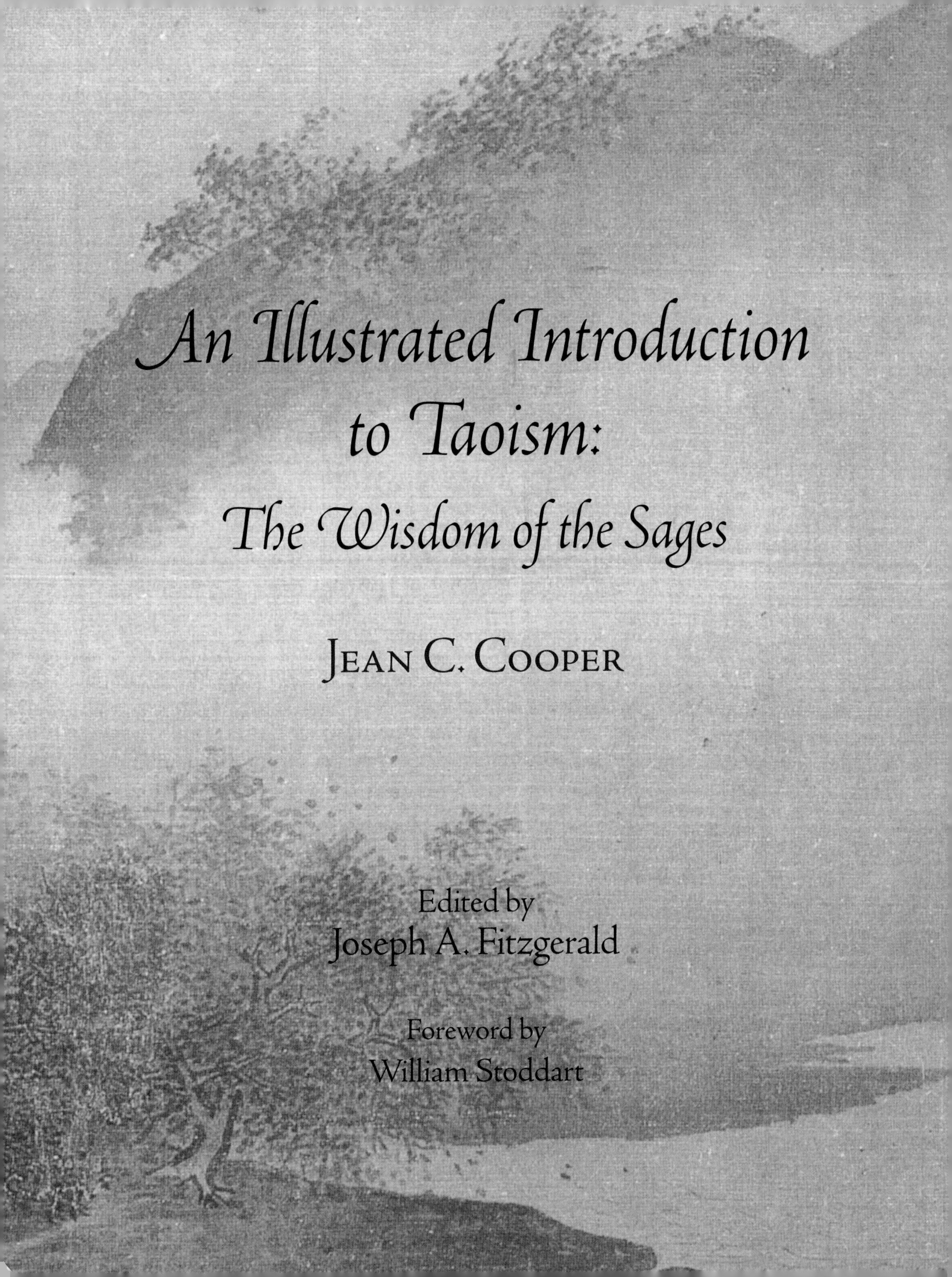

An Illustrated Introduction to Taoism:

The Wisdom of the Sages

Jean C. Cooper

Edited by
Joseph A. Fitzgerald

Foreword by
William Stoddart

An Illustrated Introduction to Taoism: The Wisdom of the Sages

Image research and book design by Susana Marín

Library of Congress Cataloging-in-Publication Data

Cooper, J. C. (Jean C.)
An illustrated introduction to Taoism : the wisdom of the sages / Jean C. Cooper ; edited by Joseph A. Fitzgerald ; foreword by William Stoddart.
p. cm. -- (Treasures of the world's religions)
Includes bibliographical references and index.
ISBN 978-1-935493-16-7 (pbk. : alk. paper) 1. Taoism. I. Fitzgerald, Joseph A., 1977- II. Title.
BL1920.C59 2010
299.5'14--dc22

2010005150

Cover image: Wall painting from the Yüan dynasty depicting the Jade Emperor, his consort, the Empress of Heaven, and Lao Tzu, the founder of Taoism.

Printed on acid-free paper in China.

For information address World Wisdom, Inc.
P.O. Box 2682, Bloomington, Indiana 47402-2682
www.worldwisdom.com

CONTENTS

Tai Chin (1388-1462), *Dense Green on Spring Mountains*, Ming dynasty

EDITOR'S PREFACE

> Forget the years, forget distinctions. Leap into the boundless and make it your home![1] —*Chuang Tzu*

In the view of Thomas Merton, Taoism is basically direct and simple in that it seeks, "as does all the greatest philosophical thought, to go immediately to the heart of things".[2] And it is straight to the heart of things that Jean Campbell Cooper takes us in her penetrating essays on the Taoist tradition and its presiding ideas.

Born in 1905 in Chefoo, China, Cooper received the indelible imprint of Taoism, Buddhism, and Confucianism. As she recalls:

> I was born in China and spent my early formative years there, my father having been in the consular service and later a director of one of the missions then operating in the country, so I was brought up by Christian parents and Taoist-Buddhist amahs [nurses], seeing more of the latter than the former. Thus, if one follows the Jesuit adage "give me a child for the first seven years", it is easy to see why those years were more influenced by Eastern than Western thought and attitudes. I also grew up with the vivid contrasts between the imported Western opulence and the squalor of the city back streets, and, against these, the breathtaking and magical beauty of the mountain country where I was sent to boarding school at an early age. Overall, too, I learned the charm of the Chinese character, with its balance between Confucian social decorum and Taoist gamin individuality as well as the beauty of the arts and crafts with which one was surrounded.[3]

Returning to England, she later studied philosophy at St. Andrew's University, and throughout the rest of her life wrote and lectured on Taoism, comparative religion, philosophy, and symbolism.[4] "My interest in writing on mysticism", Cooper relates, "is

[1] *Zhuangzi: Basic Writings*, trans. Burton Watson (New York: Columbia University Press, 2003), p. 44.

[2] Thomas Merton, *The Way of Chuang Tzu* (New York: New Directions, 1969), p. 11.

[3] *Contemporary Authors: A Bio-Bibliographical Guide to Current Writers in Fiction, General Nonfiction, Poetry, Journalism, Drama, Motion Pictures, Television, and Other Fields*, edited by Susan M. Trosky, (Detroit: Gale Research Inc., 1989), vol. 127, p. 88.

[4] Cooper's works on mythology, symbolism, and comparative religion are important in their own right. These include: *Cassell Dictionary of Christianity* (London: Cassell, 1996); *The Dictionary of Festivals* (London: Thorsons Publishers, 1996); *Dictionary of Symbolic and Mythological Animals* (London: Thorsons Publishers, 1995); *Brewer's Book of Myth and Legend* (Oxford: Helicon Publishing, 1993); *An*

to join with those who feel that the West has largely grown to ignore its heritage in this respect and is now turning to the East so that a strong East-West exchange of thought and belief has developed; those who have a foot in both camps can contribute to this dialogue."[5] The contents of this volume are gathered from three of her books which continue to be among the most reliable and accessible introductions to Taoism: *Taoism: The Way of the Mystic*, *Yin & Yang: The Taoist Harmony of Opposites*, and *Chinese Alchemy: The Taoist Quest for Immortality*.[6] While in the main they explore the distinctive contours of the Taoist spiritual landscape, these works are also notable for their author's ability to identify points of contact between Taoism and other major religions, "illustrating how, in many essential ways, they speak with one voice".[7]

Numerous images taken from Taoism's rich pictorial heritage are included herein.[8] "Traditional, or classical, Taoism", Cooper explains, "may be the most intellectual of religions or philosophies, but there is nothing one-sided about it: it involves the whole man, mentally, emotionally, and spiritually. It includes not only the wisdom of Lao Tzu and the metaphysical poetry of Chuang Tzu, but was also the inspiration for the most exquisite and evocative painting and poetry, which could range from the sublime to the humorous or caustic, and it gave birth to a civilization supreme in all the arts and crafts."[9] It may even be that some artworks have the power to convey what "cannot be conveyed either by words or by silence":[10] the transcendental nature of Tao.

May this illustrated anthology[11] of Cooper's writings offer to its readers a worthy introduction to that ever-vital wisdom of "the Sages of old".

—Joseph A. Fitzgerald

Illustrated Encyclopaedia of Traditional Symbols (London: Thames & Hudson, 1987); *Fairy Tales: Allegories of the Inner Life* (Wellingborough: Aquarian Press, 1983); and *Symbolism: The Universal Language* (Wellingborough: Aquarian Press, 1982). They are now available in some fourteen languages, including Greek, Serbo-Croat, Finnish, Japanese, and practically all western European languages.

5 *Contemporary Authors*, vol. 127, p. 88.

6 Respectively: London: Harpercollins, 1990; Wellingborough: Aquarian Press, 1981; and New York: Sterling Publishing, 1990. Her writings on Taoism have also found a considerable audience through their translation into languages such as French, Spanish, German, Portuguese, Dutch, and Swedish. In French, *La Philosophie du Tao* (Paris: Éditions Dangles, 1990); in Spanish, *El Taoísmo* (Buenos Aires: Lidiun, 1985) and *Yin y Yang: La armonía Taoísta de los opuestos* (Madrid: Éditorial Edaf, 1985); in German, *Was ist Taoismus? : der Weg des Tao—eine Einführung in die uralte Weisheitslehre Chinas* (München: Otto Wilhelm Barth, 1993); in Portuguese, *Taoísmo: o caminho do místico* (Martins Fontes: São Paulo, 1984) and *Yin-Yang: a harmonia taoísta dos opostos* (São Paulo: Martins Fontes, 1985); in Dutch, *Licht op taoïsme: de weg van de mysticus* (Katwijk aan Zee: Servire, 1997) and *Jin Jang: taoïsme en de harmonie van het leven in tegenpolen* (Katwijk aan Zee: Servire, 1989); and in Swedish, *Taoismen: en introduktion* (Stockholm: Wahlström & Widstrand, 1997).

7 *Yin & Yang*, p. 11.

8 Some of the illustrations, however, are Taoist-inspired rather than strictly Taoist.

9 *Yin & Yang*, p. 13.

10 *Chuang Tzu* XXV, trans. Herbert Giles (London: George Allen & Unwin, 1961).

11 Editorial changes include the deletion and re-ordering of certain passages; in order to facilitate readability, we have not noted such alterations within the text.

FOREWORD

Hinduism says: "God and His Name are One". Taoism says: "The Name that can be named is not the Name." Which is right? In this book, Mrs. Cooper deftly demonstrates how both of these apparently conflicting expressions of Ultimate Reality are true!

The legendary Fu-Hsi was the first of the "Three Noble Emperors" of China, who are believed to have reigned during the first part of the third millennium B.C. Fu-Hsi was the "Originator" or "Revealer" of the famous Eight Trigrams of the *I-Ching* ("The Book of Changes"), and these trigrams are said to have been the origin of the Chinese pictographic script. It is from this primordial hyperborean shamanism, known simply as the "Tradition of Fu-Hsi", that are derived both Taoism and Confucianism. This division of the ancient tradition into two branches occurred in the sixth century B.C. The specific revealer of Taoism was Lao Tzu (604-531 B.C.) and that of Confucianism was of course Confucius (551-479 B.C.).

The third Chinese religion, Buddhism, came from India. It began to be introduced into China in the first century A.D. by Indian Buddhist monks, who came, it is said, at the invitation of the mythical Emperor Fu-Hsi and Lao Tzu, each of whom was regarded as possessing immortality.

In addition to the preaching of the Indian monks, Chinese pilgrims also went to India to visit the earliest and most sacred of the Buddhist shrines and to study the teachings of Buddhism, thereafter returning to their own country to spread these teachings amongst the population. From that time onwards, one spoke of the "Three Religions", and henceforth they combined harmoniously to fashion Chinese civilization.

This combination was not simply a praiseworthy example of "inter-religious toleration"; it was because Taoism and Confucianism are both shamanisms (deriving from the ancient shamanistic Tradition of Fu-Hsi), while Buddhism is a "denomination", as are the majority of the world religions. Shamanisms, as indigenous "nature religions", offer no competition to the denominations. It is the denominations, not the shamanisms, which are in competition with each other. One cannot be a Christian and a Muslim at the same time, but (in Japan) one can be a Buddhist and a Shintoist at the same time, and (in Tibet) a Buddhist and a Bön-Po at the same time. The situation is analogous in North America, where an Indian can be a Christian without thereby abandoning the Religion of the Sun Dance and the Sacred Pipe.

One might ask: why did the Tradition of Fu-Hsi split into two parts, and what is the role of these two parts? The answer is provided by Confucius himself. On the one occasion that the two Masters met, Confucius said to Lao Tzu: "The highest rung on my ladder corresponds to the lowest rung on your ladder." In other words, Confucianism is an "exoterism" and Taoism is an "esoterism".

Confucianism teaches courtesy, good manners, and good "government" (of self, of cities, and of states). Confucianism, which is "exoteric" and social (and yet at the same time "aristocratic") is partnered by Taoism, which is "esoteric" and spiritual (and yet at the same time "popular").

As for Buddhism, it is believed and practiced throughout all the provinces of China. It is the religion of renunciation, compassion, and peace. It is the religion of *Nirvana* (the "Extinction of that which causes suffering"). The Buddha declared: "I teach two things, O disciples, suffering and release from suffering."

Of the "Three Religions", Taoism is the one least known in the West. Mrs. Cooper's lucid exposition of the doctrines and practices of this religion richly satisfies a pressing need.

—William Stoddart

Deified Lao Tzu, T'ang dynasty,
late 7th-early 8th century

INTRODUCTION

There are two main schools of thought as to the origin of Taoism. One sees it as a development of early animism and magical practices, and to support this theory there is the legend of the Yellow Emperor, living some three thousand years B.C., who was reputed to have been instructed in magic, mysticism, and love by his three Immortal Maids or Ladies. Others maintain that although the doctrine of Tao existed earlier, classical Taoism began with Li Erh, popularly known as Lao Tzu (the Old Philosopher, or the Old Boy) whose date was about 600 B.C. His philosophy was later developed by Chuang Tzu as a rarefied metaphysical teaching and a protest against magic and popular superstitions. If the Yellow Emperor studied magic in connection with the Tao it is reasonable to suppose that the element of magic, so prominent in later, decadent Taoism, was there from the beginning but was regarded as undesirable and irrelevant and therefore expunged from the teachings of Lao Tzu and Chuang Tzu. Whichever viewpoint is chosen, the fact remains that there are no authentic texts, only a few fragments, before Lao Tzu's *Tao Te Ching* and the *Book of Chuang Tzu* and that classical Taoism as it is now known is based on these writings. Never did a world philosophy rest on a smaller basis. The *Tao Te Ching*, more translated than any other book except the Bible, consists of a mere five thousand words, while Chuang Tzu's book, though containing thirty-three chapters in its present form, is thought to have been enlarged from its original seven "inner chapters" by later additions and redactions; a frequent habit with Chinese classical writers.

In the traditional Taoism of Lao Tzu and Chuang Tzu cosmology, philosophy, and religion are closely connected, but conventional standards of ethics, moral humbug, and sophistication are mocked while meaningless ritual and magic are repudiated. Taoism is the philosophy of the art of living and relationships; it deals with the whole of Nature and man's place in it. It is the philosophy of the rhythm of life and simplicity of mind and spirit together with the absence of calculated activity, as expressed in the doctrine of *wu-wei*, and the presence of spontaneity, balance and harmony. It is not a world-renouncing philosophy, but a withdrawal from all that is artificial, sophisticated and worthless; it is "to use the light within to revert to your natural clearness of sight" and "to live in contact with the world and yet in harmony with the light". It is a natural unfolding through a clarity of perception and awareness which watches but does not pre-judge or indulge in criticism and analysis, which only cause separation between the perceiver and the thing perceived.

The basic aim of the Taoist is the attaining of balance and harmony between the *yin* and the *yang*, known as the Two Great Powers, the two poles between which all manifestation takes place. This balance and harmony must be achieved both in one's self and in the world until the two are resolved into the One, but it is useless to try to impose this on the world from without; one can only reform one's self and until that self is in equilibrium and has achieved total harmlessness, both to itself and others, it can offer nothing worthwhile to the world in general. That is why both Taoism and Confucianism always taught by example. "The Sage speaks without words"; if the Sage does not radiate wisdom and the saint goodness, they can save themselves the trouble of teaching them; no one will be taken in for long. Emerson brings the same message to the West when he says: "That which we are, we shall teach, not voluntarily but involuntarily."

Both Taoism and Confucianism employ the word "Tao", the "Way", which was in use before they were founded and both refer to "the Sages of old"; but for the Confucianist the Way is ethical, while for Lao Tzu and Chuang Tzu it is metaphysical. "Never for a moment does the perfect man leave the way of virtue", would be interpreted by the Confucianist as strict conformity to *li*—that is, propriety, morality, ceremonial, principle—while for the Taoist, virtue lies not in morality but in an inward quality of obedience to the Natural, in simplicity and spontaneity. It offers no pursuit of a goal, just the Path or the Way. To pursue it is to put the object as something separate; instead of a goal there is an open-minded experience of, and absorption in, life because the Way and the Way-goer are essentially one.

Taoism frequently teaches through paradox and it is one of its paradoxes that simplicity is required to deal with the complexities of life in human nature and in one's self. To continue the paradox, simplicity is extremely difficult. It is easy to complicate things, to be involved in endless thinking, analysis, pulling to pieces, imagining, reacting to conventional ideas, prejudices, and preferences; to indulge in "something to do" or "something to think about" instead of stilling the monkey-mind, finding the futility of contrived action which leads only to separation, hardness, ethics, self-righteousness, and ultimate strife. Half the so-called problems of life are self-created by this monkey-mind in order to give it its "something to do" and to distract it from the only valid action, the *wu-wei* or motivelessness which enables it to calm itself and cease its futilities and so see itself and everything else for what it really is and to attain the balance and harmony which transcends both action and non-action and confers the ability to maintain detachment in the midst of activity and the readiness for necessary action in the state of detachment. It also grants the ability to give without depletion or diminution of power.

For Taoism man is not the measure of the universe. All living things share in, and have their place and relationships in, Nature and partake of the *yin* and the *yang*. It is the natural which should regulate all things. "The Sage follows Nature in establishing order, he does not invent principles himself." Man's position is as the mediator between the Two Great Powers, Heaven and Earth, and he should maintain the balance between them, physically, mentally, and spiritually. He is positioned in the middle point, the Mean, called in both Taoism and Buddhism the Middle Way, between the two extremes—a position which enables man to communicate with both worlds and a viewpoint from which the opposites can be seen as such in their relativity and their contrary aspects, but also in their unity. Man should bring the spiritual down to earth and raise the earth to the spiritual. This is attained by keeping the *yin* and *yang* in balance, avoiding all extremes, and establishing harmony. Not for nothing is the Mean called "the happy mean" or medium.

In Taoism, the primordial One becomes Two in creation and the Two becomes Three and so on in an ever-increasing multiplicity in the realm of phenomena and manifestation. This multiplicity is called the Ten Thousand Things, "Ten Thousand" representing the uncountable. The Tao, as the One, the All, comprising both the unique and the commonplace in the world, exists as much in the daily round and common task as in the finest expression of human genius in the arts, religion, and philosophy. It is the changeless source of endless change and transformation in Nature and the manifest world; it is the passive source of activity. As the All, the Pleroma, it is beyond the rational mind; as an object of thought it cannot comprise the thought itself, it can only be expressed symbolically, or experienced to a limited extent in supra-rational states of intuition and mysticism. It is the Unmanifest, that which has been there from all eternity and to "find" it is only to see what was already there. It cannot be properly expressed, since it is the Inexpressible; Chuang Tzu calls it *Ta T'ung*, the Great Infinite, free from all determination, free from space and time. He says it can only be understood by inference.

The One and the Many can never be separated since neither has any meaning except in relationship with the other. This is seen symbolically in weaving, with the combination of the many threads in the one pattern, the horizontal *yin* united with the vertical *yang* in the interplay of the to and fro movement, the alternating flux, which contains both the possibility and probability of inter-change and ex-change, resulting in the final unification of often apparently conflicting forces. This is well expressed by Browning in the weaving of a carpet:

> … apart, this fiery hue,
> That watery dimness, either shocks the eye,
> So blinding bright, or else offends again
> By dullness, — yet the two, set each by each,
> Somehow produce a color born of both.

There is, then, no "this" separate from "that", just as no mystical knowledge can be obtained from separateness, from the outside; it must be an entering into, a total absorption, and it is the essence of mysticism that it transcends space and time and all dualities and reveals the realm of the undifferentiated.

五年
三日
福祿壽星君衆

1. THE TAO

The poet Po Chu-i wrote,

> "Those who speak know nothing,
> Those who know keep silence."
> These words, as I am told,
> Were spoken by Lao Tzu.
> But if we are to believe that Lao Tzu
> Was himself one who knew,
> How comes it that he wrote a book
> Of five thousand words?

The Chinese character for Tao

Which is precisely the problem confronting anybody who sets out to write on Taoism. It must be an attempt to express the inexpressible, to "unscrew the inscrutable", since the Tao is the ultimate mystery, "that from which words turn back"; that which surpasses all human definitions and contingencies and all finite thought.

However, though the Tao cannot be expressed in words, silence is also inadequate. "It cannot be conveyed either by words or by silence. In that state which is neither speech nor silence its transcendental nature may be apprehended."[1] From which it follows that Taoism is a purely metaphysical and mystical religion. Other religions have their mystical aspects; Taoism *is* mysticism. Some would query whether it is a religion at all and suggest that it is pure metaphysics. Be that as it may, "Taoism" is a term used by the Western world to distinguish one of the great movements in Chinese thought. But it has no systematic teaching as in Confucianism, and no creed; it cannot be made into a set of rules to follow. It is primarily a cosmic religion, the study of the universe and the place and function of man and all creatures and phenomena in it.

The word "Tao" is always left untranslated as it is regarded as indefinable. Its import is too great to be contained in any one word. It is best understood by inference. If it is translated, it is usually called the Way. The ideograph for the Tao is made up of two radicals: the Head, or Leader, and the Feet, or Progress by Degrees. The Head denotes a principle or beginning, while the radical for the Feet carries the implication of the power of forward movement, the two together giving the suggestion of intelligent movement along a way as well as of a pupil following a master, while the combination of the Head and Feet also implies the whole man and all that is right and normal and in conformity with the laws of nature, both in being and action; but the intelligence indicated is not that of the brain

[1] *Chuang Tzu* XXV, trans. Giles (published by George Allen & Unwin).

Opposite: *The Star-lords of Good Fortune, Emolument, and Longevity*, Ming dynasty, dated 1454

or rational mind, but a supra-rational quality.

The doctrine of the Tao existed before Lao Tzu, the reputed founder of Taoism, and is sometimes ascribed to the legendary Yellow Emperor, Huang Ti (2704-2595 B.C.). Certainly both Lao Tzu and Confucius constantly refer to the Tao in connection with "the Sages of old" of China's Golden Age, and all three religions of China, including the imported Buddhism, used the word. It is possible, however, that although the term "Tao" existed before Lao Tzu, it may have contained the meaning of the Way merely in the sense of method, or correct conduct, as it remained in Confucianism, while Lao Tzu developed, and was solely concerned with, its metaphysical connotations. For him it was no limited way or method, but the transcendental First Cause, the Primordial Unity, the ineffable, the timeless, all-pervading principle of the universe, giving rise to it yet undiminished by it; supporting and controlling it; that which preceded the creation of Heaven and Earth. It is called the Absolute, the Ultimate Reality, the Nameless, the Portal of all Mystery, the Cosmic Order. Some liken it to the *Atman* of Hinduism, the "Suchness" of Buddhism, the Ain Soph of Qabbalism, or the Monad of the Greeks, that which has neither qualities nor attributes. But even such definitions are, in a sense, misleading for, in the words of the *Tao Te Ching*, "The Tao that can be expressed is not the eternal Tao, the Name that can be defined is not the unchanging Name", and Chuang Tzu says, "The very name Tao is only adopted for convenience sake.... Tao is beyond material existence.... It may be transmitted, but it cannot be received (possessed). It may be attained but cannot be seen. It exists prior to Heaven and Earth, and, indeed, for all eternity.... It is above the Zenith but is not high; it is beneath the Nadir, but it is not low. It is prior to Heaven and Earth, but is not ancient. It is older than the most ancient, but it is not old."[2] "Tao cannot be heard. Heard it is not Tao. It cannot be seen. Seen it is not Tao."[3] Of it Lieh Tzu wrote, "That which engenders all things is itself unengendered; that by which all things are evolved is itself untouched by evolution. Self-engendered, self-evolved, it has in itself the elements of substance, appearance, wisdom, strength, dispersion, and cessation. Yet it would be a mistake to call it by any of these names",[4] for "Tao makes things what they are, but is not itself a thing. Nothing can produce Tao, yet everything has Tao within it."[5]

Okakura Kakuzo writes,[6] "The Tao is the Passage rather than the Path. It is the spirit of Cosmic Change—the eternal growth which returns upon itself to produce new forms. It recoils upon itself like the dragon, the beloved symbol of the Taoists. It folds and unfolds as do the clouds. The Tao might be spoken of as the Great Transition. Subjectively it is the Mood of the Universe." "It is the principle of all energy, yet energy it is not, but merely one of its manifestations. It is the eternal principle of all life, but no life can express it, and all bodies, all material forms, are but its changing and momentary raiment."[7] Sometimes it is called "The Mother of all Things; the primordial creative cause, the self-existent source, the

[2] *Chuang Tzu* VI, trans. Fung Yu-lan (published by The Shanghai Commercial Press, 1993).

[3] *Chuang Tzu* XXII, trans. Giles.

[4] Giles, *The Book of Lieh Tzu* p. 18 (published by John Murray).

[5] *Chuang Tzu* XXII, trans. Giles.

[6] Okakura Kakuzo, *The Book of Tea* (published by Fox Duffield, New York).

[7] Emile Hovelaque, *China* (published by J.M. Dent).

Li Kung-lin (c. 1049-1106), *Lao Tzu Delivering the Tao Te Ching*, Ming dynasty

unconditioned by which all things are conditioned, for although it does not create it is the source of all creation, the animating principle of the universe; it is 'the unchanging principle which supports the shifting multiplicity.'"

In no circumstances can the Tao be thought of or used as "God"; that term is too confined, too restricted, and in any case, not permissible since Taoism is a non-theistic religion. That is not to say it is a-theistic, for the atheist is as vitally interested in the idea of God as the theist and devotes as much time and energy to writing and arguing against his existence as the theist writing for him, and both use the personal "he" for God, while the Tao is totally impersonal. Nor is there any word in Chinese which may fairly be translated "God", for *T'ien* is also completely impersonal and is "Heaven", or "The Heavens", or "The Powers that Be", as well as heaven as a state of being. Taoism is non-theistic because the limitations of the finite human mind are realized, practically and sensibly. The transcendental would no longer be transcendent if it could be described, formulated, named. "Only the limited can be understood (in individual human mode) and be expressed."[8] The unlimited cannot be positively expressed since all expression depends on formal concepts. Words can only be applied to the empirical; they are too rigid, too heavily loaded with past accretions to be able to express the subtleties of metaphysics which must, therefore, depend largely on negatives. Nor can the unlimited be adequately expressed within the realm of change, the manifest world, since it is impossible to tie down the shifting scene long enough for it to be subject to any formula before it has changed again; its infinite variety is too great to be possible of any adequate definition. St Augustine said that, even in speaking of God, to conceive of a thing is not God, but one of his effects; and Meister Eckhart said "all you can say of God is not true", while, in our time, Ramana Maharshi taught that "Consciousness is pure. It is the same as the Self which is eternal

[8] René Guénon, *Symbolism of the Cross* (published by Luzac & Co.).

Li Kung-lin (c. 1049-1106), *Gods and Immortals in an Imaginary Landscape*, Song dynasty

and unchanging. Get rid of the subject and object and Pure Consciousness will remain. Leave God alone! You do not know God. He is only what you think of him. Is he apart from you? He is that Pure Consciousness in which all ideas are formed."

So Taoism employs the negative which is the only possible means for expressing that which is beyond being. It is to strip off layer after layer until only the essential remains, but it is not to be equated with the static. The Tao is a dynamic, vital force with all the innate powers of the potential. The negative says nothing, but contains the possibility of everything. As the Tao is inexpressible in words, being no-thing-ness, yet the potential of all things, it can only be referred to by what is not: it is the non-existent containing the potential of existence; the Void; Emptiness; non-appearance; the darkness in which light is as yet unmanifest but out of which light emerges.

Non-theism not only avoids the pitfalls of anthropomorphism but puts the stress on the otherness of the divine, which, nevertheless, is not wholly transcendent but equally immanent. Western theistic thought, if not definitely anthropomorphic, is, as Giles says, "undeniably anthropopathic".[9] There is no such element in any of the three religions of China, all are too profoundly impersonal. Only in decadent Taoism and Buddhism did a pantheon of gods arise, gods to whom appeal

[9] Giles, *Taoist Teachings* (published by John Murray).

could be made and devotions offered. Not until then was there any personalization of the forces of nature into gods and, even then, they were mostly heavenly and stellar deities. The Shang-Ti of decadent Taoism was a cosmic god, later to become the incarnation of the Chief Priest of the Taoists, but before that probably symbolic of the northern regions, the Pole Star, a symbol of the fixed center (Aristotle's "point quiescent"), although Chu, the philosopher, tries even here to slide out of any personal implication by saying "Heaven is just Shang-Ti and Shang-Ti is Heaven". Shang-Ti was possibly the introduction of a demiurge to act as an intermediary between the totally impersonal and inactive Tao and the world of active creation and to combine both the aspects of the divine and the phenomenal.

There is no Creator in traditional Taoism. The operation of the Tao brings about a spontaneous creation through the interaction of the *yin-yang* principles. Even in decadence there was never an image of God in China, only of endless inferior deities. The Supreme Principle was never formalized, and popular Confucianism, in its temples, had no images at all, but retained the atmosphere of the abstract thinking of the scholar, but while Confucianism developed a strict code of ethics and social proprieties, Taoism was totally free from any dogma or systematic codes of conduct or learning. No doubt before the founding of traditional Taoism by Lao Tzu and Chuang Tzu there were prevalent animistic concepts and beliefs in some personal god or gods, but these early ideas were surpassed in the teachings of pure Taoism: the Tao cannot be subject to any limitations. As Chuang Tzu says, "Tao is without beginning, without end." It "exists by and through itself. It existed prior to Heaven and Earth, and indeed for all eternity."[10]

There was something formless yet complete,
That existed before Heaven and Earth;
Without sound, without substance.
Dependent on nothing, unchanging,
All-pervading, unfailing.[11]

It is

a thing impalpable, incommensurable,
Yet latent in it are forms.[12]

Not only are all forms latent in Tao, but all forms and everything that exists has Tao, a "way" to fulfill and each is in its own "way" unique and constantly changing, growing, developing. The manifest world is in a perpetual state of flux, of transitoriness. It is the ever-moving, ever-changing and there is nothing fixed or permanent in the phenomenal world, all its possibilities are contained in growth and only growth can reveal life. Thus in Taoism stress is placed on the existential situation. The Way is a way of life, not a school of thought, and can only be understood by being lived, hence the small amount of written material left by the early Taoists. Also there is a danger of the written work falling into the hands of anyone and being misinterpreted or becoming a rigid doctrine or being turned into a cult. Disciples can usually be depended upon to wreck the teachings of a master. With words come confusion and misunderstanding and the possibility of an endless variety of interpretations. "Measure not in words the

[10] *Chuang Tzu* XVII, trans. Giles.
[11] *Tao Te Ching* XXV, trans. A. Waley (published by George Allen & Unwin, 1934).
[12] Ibid., XLI.

immeasurable. Rise not with thoughts to the inscrutable."[13] There is also no dogma, not only as a precaution against the human tendency to take the easiest path in establishing itself in something fixed and comfortable, of its own choosing, to run on known lines and there to stay content without further effort, to stop at halfway houses instead of continuing the difficult climb to the peaks, but as an insistence on total freedom. The Way should be one of adventure in living; adventure of the spirit. For "Life is not created: it is. Spirit cannot be commanded; it blows as it lists. Those who believe it possible to teach inspiration and genius, to enclose beauty, virtue, and truth in formulae, to impose from without what can only be born from within, are blind; the illumination of the spirit, the revelation of the Tao has never enlightened them. Each man must find in himself his own truth, his own beauty, his own virtue; the salvation of the soul, like genius, can neither be bought nor taught. Everything is unique, though the essence of all things is one. All undergo perpetual change, perpetual creation."[14] Though in its absolute sense the Tao is the indefinable, the inexpressible, in the relative world it becomes every manifestation of the power of the universe; the power which gives rise to the mutable.

One states that the Tao is inexpressible and then proceeds to say a good deal about it, just as the mystics of all religions say their experience is inexpressible and then fill volumes expressing it, often with a considerable degree of success. But what is being conveyed is that the experience is existential, involving the whole man; it is not merely an intellectual or emotional conception using a part of him. It is a living, not a theoretical, approach. But although existential, Taoism has nothing in common with the gloomy nihilism of the modern existentialism which is based on despair and expressed in anguish of mind which is the very opposite of the calm, spiritual acceptance of the existential situation rooted in the Tao. "Anguish", "dread", and "*Sorge*" have no place in the mind of one totally committed to the Way. The Way is one of joyousness, of an open-hearted acceptance of life which regards the universe as basically good and which also rejects puritanism as an aberration and a denial of the fullness of life. The wise man does not close his eyes to the beauty of the world around him, but is not, on the other hand, distracted by its merely sensual attractions. Beauty is an aid to spirituality, it is the gentle, feminine, *yin* aspect of the spiritual life, as truth is the penetrating, forceful, *yang* aspect. Both should be productive of a deep appreciation of, and joy in, life. Taoism as based on the Lao Tzu aphorisms and the works of Chuang Tzu is a Way permeated with joyousness, laughter, and wit. There is a legend that the originators of the three great religions of China stood around a jar of vinegar, the symbol of life itself, and each in turn dipped a finger into the jar to taste its content. Confucius pronounced it sour, to the Buddha it was bitter, but Lao Tzu found it sweet. Certainly Taoists were laughter-loving and in their writings and sayings the sword of discrimination is wielded with ruthless vigor as a weapon of trenchant wit, a wit which, to change the metaphor, also moves as a cleansing and winnowing wind through all Taoist texts, blowing away the accumulated dusty chaff and leaving the golden grain.

Some find a similarity in teaching in Tao-

[13] *Dhammapada.*

[14] Hovelaque, *China.*

The Vinegar Tasters, Confucius, Buddha, and Lao Tzu, hanging scroll, China

ism and Hinduism and, indeed, there was a tradition that Lao Tzu had traveled to India and even further. There is certainly a strong Brahmanical flavor in the Taoist doctrines of non-violence and the creative principle of joy at work in the universe. The *Upanishads* teach that effort can only become effective through joy. Joyousness is a power which dispels all the ills of egoism, of fear, of separation—all things which make man ineffective. It replaces these with a zestful appreciation of life. This, too is associated with the play of the universe, the play of Nature which is born of an overflowing exuberance and open-handed generosity. But there is no capriciousness in this play, it is exuberantly creative; it is to have life and to have it more abundantly. Nor must this joy be mistaken for an emotion. It is the working of the spirit in creation, not the usually accepted idea of a feeling of happiness as opposed to sorrow. Sorrow and happiness are, on the contrary, the "great heresies". "Because men are made to rejoice and sorrow and to displace their center of gravity, they lose their steadiness and are unsuccessful in thought and action", since "when man rejoices greatly he gravitates toward the positive pole. When he sorrows deeply he gravitates towards the negative."[15] This has the effect of disturbing "the equilibrium of positive and negative". So that the cultivation of the extreme in either striving for happiness as an end in itself, or the deliberate indulgence in grief, is not in conformity with the Way. Joy is the natural spiritual result of living in accord with the Tao. As Wordsworth puts it, "With an eye made quiet by the power of harmony, and the deep power of joy, We see into the life of things."[16]

The Tao is the realm of man's true being. "Tao is the Way and the goal. It is the light that sees and is sought, even as *Brahman*, in the *Upanishads*, is the principle of search as well as the object sought, the animating ideal and its fulfillment. The Spirit which moves us to seek the Truth is the Truth which we seek."[17]

[15] *Chuang Tzu* XI, trans. Giles.

[16] Wordsworth, "Tintern Abbey".

[17] S. Radhakrishnan, *India and China*.

2. *TE*

The *Tao Te Ching* is sometimes called the "Book of Lao Tzu" and has always been attributed to him, though scholars have thrown doubt on so early a date as the sixth century B.C. for its origin. Neither Ssu-ma Ch'ien nor Chuang Tzu, Lao Tzu's greatest disciple, refers to the book, although Chuang Tzu quotes and uses many passages occurring in it. Doubts have also been cast on the historical existence of Lao Tzu himself, but though little is known of him, recent scholarship accepts the *Tao Te Ching* as the work of Lao Tzu who taught and gave rise to the tradition associated with his name. He was one Li Erh, who lived for a long time in the state of Chou, about 600 B.C., but is always known by the popular name of Lao Tzu, "Lao" being "old" and "Tzu" a courtesy title conferred upon great sages or authors of classics. "Old" carries a tone of affection with it and so he could just as well be called the Old Master, or the Old Boy, and we get the impression of a genial, kindly, laughter-loving sage. The exaggerated value placed on historicity by the West does not obtain in the East where it is regarded as largely irrelevant. All that matters is the doctrine taught, not who, precisely, originated it.

Lao Tzu copy of *Tao Te Ching*, excavated from a Western Han dynasty tomb at Mawangdui, Changsha, Hunan province, 3rd century

Legend has it that as Lao Tzu left the active world for retirement in the mountains of the far west, the Frontier Warden asked him to pause for a while and write a book containing his teachings. The result was a book on the Tao and the *Te*, the Way and its Virtue. Lao Tzu then travelled over the high pass and was seen no more. But whatever the origin of the book, it remains a perpetual challenge to metaphysicians and translators alike and it has been the foundation stone and accepted canon of Taoism. Next to the Bible the *Tao Te Ching* is the most translated book in the world. It is certainly the most baffling and enigmatic.

The addition of "*Ching*" to any work means that it is regarded as a classic or canon; it is a complimentary title given to books held in great veneration.

Te, usually translated as "Virtue", is the "uprightness" symbolized by a straight line indicating the Tao, or Way, which is a conformity to principles and which also symbolizes the *axis mundi*. *Te* is, in a sense, Tao made manifest, the revelation of the true nature of the Tao. Although occasionally employed to signify conventional virtue, the true meaning

Shang Hsi (active early 15th century), *Lao Tzu meeting Yin Hsi at the Hanku Pass*, Ming dynasty

is the quality of natural goodness which is the result of enlightenment and of the manifestation and function of the Tao in man and all that exists in the universe.

This "virtue" has no moral overtones; it is an inward quality in man and all creatures, a potentiality and latent natural power arising from and dependent on the Tao, from which it is an emanation. Chuang Tzu defines it as "the perfect attainment of harmony",[1] and says that "there is nothing more fatal than intentional virtue, when the mind looks outward".[2] It is sometimes suggested that the moral and ethical is ignored or neglected in Taoism, but this is a misunderstanding. There is no emphasis on morality because it is taken for granted; the stage of ethics is already surpassed. The Sage, the living example of the *Te*, is not a "moral" man since morals do not enter into his mind. He is already so perfectly adjusted and in such complete harmony with his surroundings that he acts with spontaneous perfection, far beyond any thou shalt, thou shalt not, and all relative morality is adapted to the particular situation. "The Sage has no deficiency in his character and therefore needs no morality."[3] "He who knows the Tao is sure to understand how to regulate his conduct in all varying circumstances. Having that understanding he will not allow things to injure himself ... nothing can injure him."[4] Conscious virtue appears only in an already "fallen" society and is symptomatic of spiritual malaise. Perfect simplicity and naturalness belong to the primordial and paradisal state of the Tao. "Wherefore, when Tao is lost, virtue comes, when virtue is lost comes benevolence,

[1] *Chuang Tzu* V, trans. Fung Yu-lan.
[2] *Chuang Tzu* XXXII, trans. Giles.
[3] *Chuang Tzu* V, trans. Fung Yu-lan.
[4] *Chuang Tzu* XVLL, trans. J. Legge (from *The Texts of Taoism*, published by Julian Press, New York).

when benevolence is lost there is justice, when justice is lost there are the rules of conduct."[5]

No other system exposes and ridicules moral sham more ruthlessly or with more zest and humor. "To employ goodness as a passport to influence … is an everlasting shame."[6] It is useless to preach morality and charity and all the conventional virtues "before reaching the heart of the example of one's own disregard for name and fame",[7] and, after listening to a pious dissertation on the virtues of self-sacrifice and charity, Lao Tzu exclaims, "What stuff! Is not your elimination of self a positive manifestation of self?"[8] Virtue must also be an inward quality. "Unless there is a suitable endowment within, Tao will not abide. Unless there is outward correctness Tao will not operate."[9] The possessor of true virtue has no air of smugness about him, nor does he criticize others. "The truly great man, although he does not injure others, does not credit himself with charity and mercy.… He asks help from no man, but takes no credit for his self-reliance.… He acts differently from the vulgar crowd, but takes no credit for his exceptionality; nor because others act with the majority does he despise them as hypocrites."[10] Conventional morality is so much a matter of opinion and relativeness, circumstances altering cases, there always being modifying circumstances in every individual case, that morality, like everything else in the phenomenal world, is subject to the principle of "universal reversibility"

[5] *Tao Te Ching* XXXVIII, trans. Giles.
[6] *Chuang Tzu* XIII, trans. Giles.
[7] Ibid., IV.
[8] Ibid., XIII.
[9] Ibid., XIV.
[10] Ibid., XVII.

The virtue of *Te* is what Aquinas would regard as an intellectual, rather than a moral, quality, since it leads to knowledge and understanding, while moral virtues are more a matter of the will. Properly understood, the intellectual virtues must lead to wisdom, and thus right action becomes a natural and inevitable corollary.

Taoism has no doctrine of sin. Ethics should be incidental to spiritual values, and, indeed, there is no ideograph in Chinese which conveys the Western conception of sin and a sense of guilt. Sin is ignorance, or stupidity, or plain lunacy, since no one in his right senses would wittingly do that which would bring automatic retribution and so injure himself. Contravention of the laws of nature brings inevitable punishment; the violent man comes to a violent end; the indulgent man first vitiates, then kills, his own appetites; the man who battens on or hurts his fellow men turns society against himself. Sin is, for the Taoist, rather a violation of the harmony of the universe than any personal infringement of a divine command and as such it creates disharmony and, therefore, disquiet in the individual in particular and thence in society in general. An ethical life is assumed as a precondition for normal life: there is not thought to be any alternative, for a manner of life which ignored the moral obligations of man to his fellow men and himself would disturb the balance of both his own character and the world about him. What, in theistic religions, is an obligation to conform to the will of God is, in Taoism, a natural co-operation with the harmony of the universe. The fundamental law and order of the Tao governs the whole cosmos, and to this man must conform if he is to fulfill his potential and play his part in maintaining cosmic harmony. The animal and plant world

Opposite: Wang E (c. 1462-after 1541), *Crossing a Bridge to Visit a Friend*

松下碧
設窗
方下榻
徐孺過
申仲夏月
題

Wu Wei (1459-1508), *Discussing the Tao*, Ming dynasty

conform "naturally", by instinct; only man chooses to maintain or destroy the balance.

Ignorance is at the root of man's moral malaise; it is his lack of knowledge and understanding of his true nature and its identity with the Tao. Ignorance identifies him with the impressions of the senses, imagining them to be the sum total of experience and knowledge, confusing the body with the power which works in and through it and setting up a chain of false values. With sin regarded as ignorance rather than disobedience to divine command, man is relieved of the guilt complex which so bedevils the Western mind.

The laying down of hard and fast rules of morality and conduct is deprecated as being rigid and destroying spontaneity. A code of laws gives a false sense of security; one has merely to follow it and all seems well, but, in the ever-changing situation of life, rigidity is death. The stable guiding-lines of custom lull man into feeling that all is well without, while all may be ill within. For the wise man morality becomes an inward judgment of wisdom. "The man who has wisdom does not sin, he ceases to do evil and through his wisdom annuls the evils of his former life."[11]

Confucianism has a strict moral code, but it arose from a profound sense of decorum and operated for the smooth conduct of both ceremonial state occasions and the everyday life of the people, but Taoism and Confucianism join in maintaining that there is nothing inherently evil in the universe. Thus neither has a doctrine of original sin and its corollary, vicarious redemption. Still less is there the idea of total corruption and damnation of souls. There is also no close personal relationship between man and deity, and no exclusive-

[11] *Mahabharata* XII, 273, 20.

ness of a chosen people or an elect, be it a race or an individual. "Weal and woe are not predestined, men bring them on themselves. The reward of good and evil follow as shadow follows substance."[12] This was realized by a young successor to the T'ang throne, who started life with a continual round of self-indulgence but soon saw the mistake he was making and said, "There is no escape from the calamities brought down by oneself", and forthwith changed his mode of life.

Remorse is totally alien to the atmosphere of Taoism. The word means "to bite again" and implies a deliberate keeping open of the wound, which is a subtle and morbid form of egoism and strengthens rather than decreases the ego. Remorse, passionate repentance, sudden conversion of the evangelical type, where the change is purely emotional and unaccompanied by any increase in wisdom and understanding, are all violent emotions and therefore out of harmony with nature and the quiet and steady development of wisdom.

It follows that there is also nothing equivalent to the idea of consecration, of setting apart, of holiness, no prayer for forgiveness (for how can one condescendingly "forgive" that which is part and parcel of one's own nature, as all men and creatures are?). There is no sacrifice to obtain pardon, no prophetic element, which is bound up with anthropomorphism, and no prayers for personal favors. Any prayer must be for guidance to carry out the Will of Heaven. In the ritual "sacrifices" at the solstices the emperor, as officiant, did not act the role of propitiator, but put himself in touch with Heaven to learn its will and to offer gratitude for former guidance. The decree of Heaven was the mandate of the king or emperor (the term "Emperor" was not used until approximately 100 B.C.) to rule the kingdom, but he forfeited this divine right as soon as he failed to act in accordance with the Will of Heaven. So, too, ordinary man had to "justify" himself before Heaven, but favors could not be bought, nor could Heaven be influenced by sacrifices. Correct conduct was the means of putting both king and subject into conformity with the Will of Heaven and so producing harmony in all relationships in the universe. There was no possibility of vicarious sacrifice. "Sacrifice does not consist merely of material objects which are only external. Essentially it consists in that which comes from the innermost living heart…, hence only the good man is able to offer sacrifice properly."[13] As Ross comments in *The Original Religion of China*, "The root of sacrifice is the heart.… It means that man entertains in his heart no desire which is out of harmony with his true self and that his outward life is in complete accord with the Tao.… He seeks from sacrifice no personal gain, no private advantage."

Original Taoism had no Hell, no Devil, no wholly dark, evil forces in direct conflict with a God of light and good; there was nothing intrinsically "diabolical" in the universe. Equally there was no Heaven of rewards: Taoist doctrines excluded all extremes of pleasure and pain. Heaven and Hell, such as they are, are, like Virtue, an inward quality and state. To do right is to obey the laws of Nature, of Virtue, and to live in conformity and harmony with them. Failure to do so brings automatic and equally natural retribution, disharmony, disruption, and consequent misery. Heaven is just as bound by these ordinances as is man, in view of the mutual interdependence of all things.

[12] *Kan Ying P'ien*, Taoist treatise of action.

[13] *The Book of Ritual.*

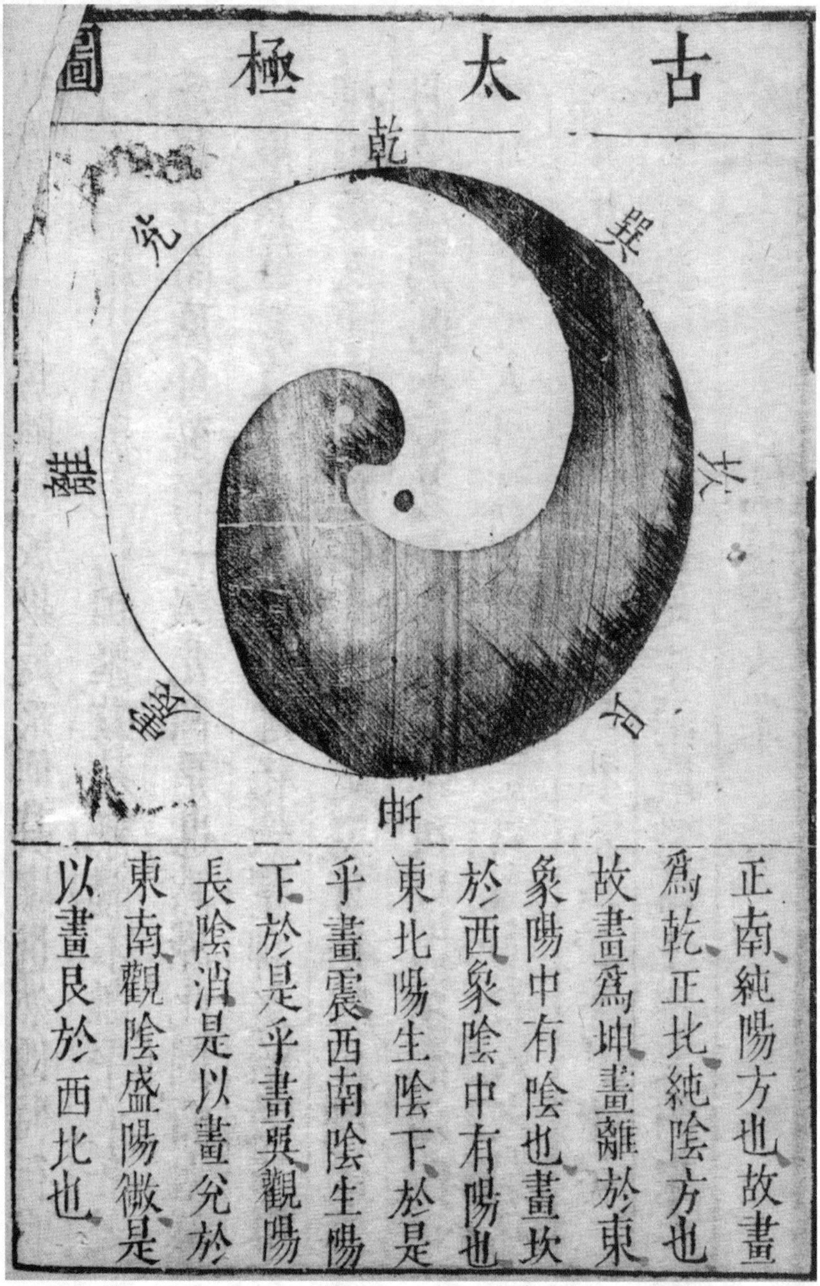

Diagram of the Supreme Ultimate, from the *Compendium of Diagrams*, compiled by the scholar Chang Huang (1526-1608), Ming dynasty, c. 1623

3. *YIN-YANG*

Perhaps the best known symbol of the Far East is the *yin-yang*, also known as the *Ti* and *T'ien*, Earth and Heaven, the principle of dualism in the manifest world. It is not exclusively Taoist or Confucianist in origin, though it is used throughout by both, but was adopted from a philosophy anterior to both. Together with the *Pa Kua* it was attributed to Fu-hsi, the first recorded Chinese ruler (2852-2738 B.C.) and it became basic to both philosophies, admirably suiting the Chinese temperament and turn of mind. But in Taoism it became the cosmic symbol of primordial unity and harmony and manifest phenomenal duality, or, as Chuang Tzu calls it, the symbol of "The Two Powers of Nature", the two great regulating forces of cosmic order in the phenomenal world.

The *yin-yang* diagram shows the two great forces of the universe, the dark and light, negative and positive, female and male, to be held in complete balance and equality of power; together they control everything in the realm of manifestation. There is a point, or embryo, of black in the white and white in the black. This is not fortuitous, but essential to the symbolism, since there is no being which does not contain within itself the germ of its opposite. There is no male wholly without feminine characteristics and no female without its masculine attributes, otherwise the dualities would forever remain in watertight compartments and the whole power of interaction be lost. Wisdom and Method would eternally be divorced and die of inanition instead of combining in the mutual "play" of creation which is responsible for the birth of the phenomenal world and which will ultimately bring it back to unity. The two forces are mutually interdependent and neither can stand alone nor be complete in itself. The two completely balanced powers are held together in the all-embracing circle of unity and the whole figure symbolizes the primordium.

The *yin-yang* symbolism is completely free from any vestige of anthropomorphism or theriomorphism, and although it is feminine-masculine the sexual aspect is the last and least to be emphasized. The realm in question is the metaphysical first and, by analogy, the mental and physical. It is a realm of relationships and it is this essentially creative duality of the *yin-yang* that gives rise to this state and all the balance of opposites and complementary qualities of the phenomenal world. It is necessary to have a pair for any form of relationship and creation. These give rise to further forms of life, again whether physical, mental, or spiritual. For anything to be able to be conceived or thought or perceived in the manifest world there must be a relationship. It is of this that Chuang Tzu says, "The perfect negative principle is majestically passive. The perfect positive is powerfully active.... The interaction of the two results in that harmony by which all things are produced."[1]

The dualism of the *yin-yang* is not radical. Although sometimes called "The Great

[1] *Chuang Tzu* XXI, trans. Giles.

Extremes", any opposition is merely apparent; the actuality is a "harmonious unity". They are not two absolute and irreconcilable opposing forces, as in absolutely dualistic philosophies and religions which deny any possibility of ultimate resolution in a transcendent unity; they are the different aspects of the whole; the two sides of one coin. They are at one and the same time a division and a reunion, and if they are spoken of as contending forces, they are also co-operating powers and the tension in which they are held is that of harmony, of the mutual play of creation, not of conflict. There is no Creator in Taoism, but the operation of the Tao brings about a spontaneous creation through the interaction of the *yin* and the *yang*.

The *yin-yang* symbolizes all paired existence, the complementary poles of nature, but the two are not to be taken as substances or entities, but as qualities inherent in all things. Between them there is perpetual and reciprocal action and reaction, interdependence and mutation, a fusion of so-called opposites. They are there "of necessity". They partake of all the symbolism of contrary yet co-operating forces. The two diagrams show the powers first in their immutable, absolute form, which in its entirety represents the Tao, and secondly as movable and relative, in perpetual alternation, or, as René Grousset puts it, in "universal reversibility".[2]

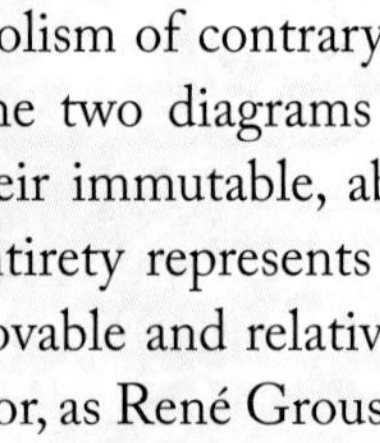

Yin-Yang. Immutable. Absolute

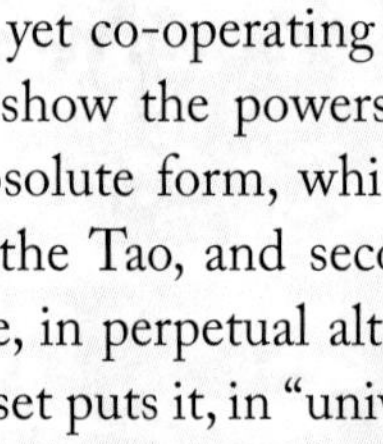

Yin-Yang. Movable. Relative.

[2] René Grousset, *The Rise and Splendour of the Chinese Empire*.

The *yin* principle is the negative, dark side and also symbolizes the feminine element, which is the potential, the existential, the natural. It is the primordial chaos of darkness from which the phenomenal world emerged into the light of creation, but this chaos is not to be equated with the Tao, which is pre-chaos. The *yin* is the eternally creative, feminine, the Great Mother, which is why the *yin* is always placed before the *yang*, since the *yang* was born of the potential and is the light which emerged from the darkness to become the actual, the essential, the spirit or Intellect.

Chuang Tzu speaks of *yin* as "Repose, the influence of the negative" and *yang* as "Motion, the power of the positive". The one is inertia, contraction, condensation, retreat; the other expansion, dispersion, advance. But with their perpetual interaction each can, and does, give rise to its opposite. Birth from the feminine principle results in death and death gives rise to new life. Light, born of darkness, grows then fades into darkness again, from which the new dawn arises. The *yin* principle controls the cold, dark, northern, winter region and the western moon, while to the *yang* belongs the warm, light, southern, summer and the eastern sun. The two together are also waning and waxing, going and coming, closing and opening, all in the process of transformation and change. "Whenever a climax is reached, there is transformation, there is an effective evolving. Wherever there is effective evolving there is a continuous survival."[3]

In one sense the contraries are complementary and co-operative, in another they are mutually destructive or exclusive just as light and darkness cannot exist without eliminating

[3] *Hsi Tz'u*, trans. Fung Yu-lan.

each other, but the existence of each is only possible in juxtaposition to the other. There is a two-way traffic of similarity and dissimilarity, there are complementary qualities but also tensions and a pull in the opposite direction, but it is a tension of balance and not of antagonism and, as seen in the alchemical symbolism, the opposites can transform each other. Creation as we know it can only take place in situations of interactions of opposites, but "all contraries cease to exist as such at the moment one views them from a higher level than the one where their opposition has its reality". The basis of transformation and transmutation is the acceptance of the whole with its negative and positive aspects. The *via negativa* works through rejection of things that are not, *neti*, *neti*, not this, not that, and the positive plays its complementary part in the acceptance of things as they are, not as it is imagined or hoped they may be. This is the basis of Taoist alchemy, working on both aspects, accepting and using their complementary diversity in the work of transmutation of the individual parts into the whole, the One.

It is accepted that the negative and positive powers can, and do, change places on different levels, such as the emotional plane in which the feminine aspect assumes the positive and the masculine becomes negative; change takes place from level to level, both upwards and downwards. We also see the give-and-take of the coincidence of opposites in the Many and the One; the One gives rise to the Many and the Many finally dissolves into the One; thesis gives rise to antithesis, each implying, requiring, and acting on the other until the final synthesis. Everything in dualism is a reflection of the One, the Real. As the moon borrows light from the sun, so manifestation borrows its existence from that which is beyond it and ultimately unifies it. The relative world shines with the light of the Absolute.

So deeply does the *yin-yang* symbolism penetrate that it is carried into all forms of life and the entire setting of man. It must be appreciated at all different levels, from the vastness of the universe to the close intimacy of the home and to all the ramifications of the plant and animal kingdoms. The *yin* is the mother aspect, mercy and wisdom, extending from the lowest and humblest peasant to the serene and all-embracing compassion and motherhood of the Moon Mother, the Queen of Heaven, represented, in China, by

Hsi Wang Mu, the Queen Mother of the West, a divine personification of *yin*, Yüan dynasty

Yen Li-pen (600-673), *Ts'ao P'i, Emperor of Wei*, T'ang dynasty

Kwan-yin. The *yang*, the father aspect, is justice and method and the power of the Sun. Man's nature must also be held in the *yin-yang* balance of intellect and feeling. "There must be human-heartedness as well as wisdom." The feminine is the passive, receptive, and soft, and in the body is represented by the flesh, while the masculine is the active, aggressive, and hard, and in the body is the bone. The north side of a valley, or anywhere in the shade, is *yin*, and the south side, or any sunny place, is *yang*. In the home the house is *yang*, built of hard, dry stone, and the garden is the *yin* principle with the soil and the water of the fish-pond or fountain or lake representing the earth and humid aspect as well as the quality of repose and receptivity, while the interactivity of the two forces is shown in the clear surface of the water receiving and giving back the light of the sun.

The *yin* and *yang* also control the seasons of the year, for autumn, the time of retreat of the life forces, and winter, when the earth is "closed", lying fallow, passive, cold, untouched and sacred, are *yin*. Spring, when the earth is "opened" to the warmth of heaven by the

Left: *Chu Shu-chung, Autumn Mountains*, Yüan dynasty, 1365
Right: *A Lofty Scholar Playing the Lute*, attributed to Jen Jen-fa (1255-1328), Yüan dynasty

plough, and summer, when the generative growing power of the sun is at its height, are *yang*. The harvest festival closed the year with the emperor, as the son of Heaven, himself symbolizing the combined powers of *yin* and *yang* as the supreme temporal and spiritual power, conducting the ceremonies. In spring the first furrow was ploughed ritually by the emperor in the "opening" ceremony. The summer solstice was ritually celebrated on the square altar of Earth, symbolized by a square yellow stone, as the time of the approach of the cold and darkness of winter to the earth. The winter solstice, at the change of the year, with the increasing power of the sun and the coming of warmth, was celebrated on the altar of Heaven, its symbol a round, blue jade stone.

The open altar at the Temple of Heaven, Beijing

Another symbol of the *yin* is the square of the earth, with the circle of the heavens representing the *yang*. In the Imperial Palaces at Peking, the great Altar of Heaven was round and open to the sky, as a symbolic testimony to the fact that the Supreme Power is open to all under heaven; the Altar of Earth was square and enclosed, the enclosure representing the protective womb aspect of the feminine principle. The roundness of the *yang* symbolizes movement, dynamism and creativity, while the square is the static and passive.

The two indigenous religions of China were in themselves *yin-yang* forces in the life of the people and helped to maintain it in balance. Taoism supplied the creative, artistic, and mystic element, while Confucianism was responsible for the social order, decorum, and ritual. Taoism is based on rhythm and flux, on the natural, the unconventional, the freedom-loving detachment from worldly things and its product is the poet, the artist, the metaphysician, the mystic, together with all that is laughter-loving and light-hearted. Confucianism is concerned with the stable order, the formal, the conventional, and the practical administration of worldly affairs; the one idealistic, the other realistic, but together the perfect combination offsetting and correcting each other and preventing too unconstrained an informalism on the one side or too arid and rigid a classicism on the other.

The Perfect Man, or Sage, so frequently referred to in both Taoist and Confucianist writings, was in himself a perfect *yin-yang* harmony. "In repose he shares the passivity of the *yin*, in action the energy of the *yang*."[4] He possessed a balance of head and heart, mind and emotions, intelligence and instinct. He is neither negative nor positive, but the happy mean, the central axis, the pole.

By itself, the critical, rational, analyzing mind is prone to *hubris*, it names, defines, and limits, and mistaking the naming of a thing for the understanding of it, sees itself as all-powerful and all-wise. The feelings, uncontrolled by mind, tend to dispersal and dissipation, while mind, unmodified by feeling, produces hardness and petrifaction. Today we have examples of this disastrous divorce between mind and emotions in the arid intellec-

[4] *Chuang Tzu* XV, trans. Giles.

Female and male deities representing the Moon and the Sun, 11th century handscroll

tualism of a so-called intelligentsia on the one hand and the morbid over-interest in sensation and sexualism on the other.

As feeling and mind the *yin-yang* is also being and thought. The feminine, instinctive, intuitional, and emotional is also depth, as the masculine, intelligence, rational is height. Each should inform and reconcile the other. The *yin* principle rises from rest, the *yang* is generated by motion. Chuang Tzu speaks of "the motionless grandeur" of the *yin* and "rampant, fiery vigor" of the *yang*, the one being incapable of full existence and functioning without the other. They are the ever-alternating and inseparable modes of passivity and activity, inertia and energy of the primordial power in creation, which must continue without cessation in the manifest world. Although any pair of opposites may be expressed in terms of *yin-yang*, the symbolism is essentially that of the creative process and the duality inherent in all phenomena. It is also the image of completion and wholeness, the primordial equilibrium, the Tao. As René Guénon says, "Every manifest being participates in the two principles … but in different proportions and always with one or the other predominating. The perfectly balanced union of the two terms can be realized only in the primordial state."[5] This is the state attained by the Sage. The symbol is a perpetual reminder to man that he must achieve and maintain this pristine harmony, the establishment of which is the main purpose of life.

Another name for the *yin-yang* is "The Two Essences". The essences emerge from the First Principle, the Tao, which, working in and through all things, is responsible for change, mutations, and all transformation. It is essentially concerned with the rhythms of life; it is the "perfectly balanced union" which establishes an inner harmony in man and the universe, so that man becomes at peace with himself and the world about him, with the world within and the world without. It renders him harmless both to others and himself. It produces the Perfect Man of Confucianism and the Sage of Taoism.

In the rhythms of life the interactions of the *yin-yang* are also responsible for rest and unrest, solitude and quest, the life of the hermit in the mountains and the work of the administrator in the world. Wen T'ien-siang, a statesman-sage, who was killed by Kublai Khan because of his loyalty to the last of the Sung emperors, wrote of the *yin-yang* as,

Heaven and Earth,
Which, commingled, are lodged in all beings
and flow through them.

It is not possible to think of the Two Essences as "good" or "bad" in connection with light and darkness. Neither can exist except in relationship with the other. "Those who would have right without its correlative wrong … do not apprehend the great principles of the universe, nor the conditions to which all creation is subject. One might as well talk of the existence of heaven without that of earth, or the negative principles without the positive, which is clearly absurd.… If we say that anything is good or evil because it is either good or evil in our eyes, then there is nothing which is not good, nothing which is not evil."[6] In this connection it is of interest to note the imbalance of Western thought which lays more stress on the one half of a whole than the other. To speak of a "positive" attitude, a "positive" good, is to praise it, while to say the opposite or to accuse anyone of being "negative" is to imply blame, as if, for example, electricity could function on a positive wire only. Situations can arise when a purely positive, aggressive attitude is out of place and has unfortunate results, whereas a negative, conciliating approach would meet the needs of the case. Balance requires that each should be used in its proper place with flexibility and interchangeableness. It is the "proper place" which is important where relativity holds sway. What may appear good to one is clearly bad to another. A characteristic comment from Chuang Tzu illustrates this point: "Monkey mates with monkey; the buck with the doe. Mao Ch'iang and Li Chi were considered by men to be the most beautiful of women, but at the sight of them fish dived deep in the water, birds soared up in the air, and deer hurried away. Among these four, who knows the right standard of beauty?"[7] Taoism does not make the psychological mistake of concentrating on the aspect of good only, for to ignore the dark

[5] Guénon, *Symbolism of the Cross.*

[6] *Chuang Tzu* XVII, trans. Giles.

[7] *Chuang Tzu* II, trans. Fung Yu-lan.

Opposite: *A Sage*, attributed to Liang K'ai, mid 13th century

Scholars Study the Yin-Yang, Ming dynasty, 17th century

aspect is to leave man defenceless in the fact of the dark side of nature and of himself. He must recognize fully both forces and accept and integrate them. As A. K. Coomaraswamy says, "The Supreme Identity is no less Death and a Darkness than Life and a Light."[8] All alternatives originate and exist mutually in one another and operate also in the mysterious law of the attraction of opposites and likes which works right through the realm of duality. Virtue is only known in its opposition to vice; day would not be known as such without night. Each aspect is not only complementary but inevitable. The very assertion of a negative implies its opposite, a positive. Once any quality is named and affirmed, its opposite is

[8] A.K. Coomaraswamy, *Contemporary Indian Philosophy* (ed. Radhakrishnan, published by George Allen & Unwin, 1952).

automatically called into being; duality is then created. In traditional Chinese symbolism all symbols of light and darkness are balanced and complementary.

With the principle of change in the operation of the *yin-yang* goes also the principle of reversal, the "universal reversibility". The Tao is immutable, unchanging, absolutely pure, but once in manifestation, in the realm of duality, good can change to evil and evil to good. Either can rise to a peak point and come down on the other side, thus giving rise to its opposite. There is nothing absolute in the phenomenal world, love can turn to hatred, happiness and sorrow are easily interchangeable, high and low can be reversed.

"To be" and "not to be" arise mutually,
Difficult and easy are mutually realized.
Long and short are mutually contrasted …
Before and after are in mutual sequence.

To illustrate the ease with which good and bad, fortune and misfortune can change places, Lieh Tzu gives the delightful allegory of the poor old man who lived with his son in a ruined fort at the top of a hill. He owned a horse which strayed off one day, whereupon the neighbors came to offer sympathy at his loss. "What makes you suppose that this is misfortune?" the old man asked. Later the horse returned accompanied by several wild horses and this time the neighbors came to congratulate him on his good luck. "What makes you think this is good luck?" he enquired. Having a number of horses now available, the son took to riding and, as a result, broke his leg. Once more the neighbors rallied round to express sympathy and once again the old man asked how they could know that this was misfortune. Then the next year war broke out and because he was lame the son was exempt from going to the war.

Most evils are man-made and could be man-cured; other troubles, regarded as natural, are capable of misinterpretation if only the outward appearance is considered. Once man understands their real nature they become truly "natural".

There is no clear-cut either/or, none of the hard and fast black-or-white attitude in Eastern metaphysics as there is in Western logic which rises from Aristotle's *tertium non datur*, "there is no third"; although as Tennyson said: "Nothing worth proving can be proven, nor yet disproven".[9] In Taoism there is always the third and reconciling element. This is why there is luck in odd numbers: this saying, now merely a superstition for most people, is the vestigial remains of an ancient truth. Even numbers, which belong to the *yin,* are weak because they have no center, while any odd, or *yang* number, when divided, has a center remaining. Anything divided or broken introduces an element of disorder and diversity and it is only by virtue of the Triad and its central point, the point of equilibrium, that this diversity can be restored to unity and its original harmony. Three is the first odd number and nine, which is three by three, is symbolically "the fullness of the *yang*".

Again, the Western mind is inclined to lay undue emphasis on the value of the objective; praise is reserved for an "objective attitude" while condemnation is implied in calling anything "merely subjective". What can, in fact, be completely objective? Even if some segment of knowledge or experience is shared or factual its impact on the individual is subjective. It is impossible to be absolutely objective

[9] *The Ancient Sage.*

in most of the things that matter, such as love, devotion, the beautiful; analysis immediately kills natural response. On the other hand excess of subjectivity produces egocentricity and sentimentality. Both aspects need to be held in balance. In attempting to be wholly objective one stands back and looks at the experience or event, stopping the natural flow of awareness and indulging in theorizing or criticism, becoming an onlooker, out of the flow of life: in complete subjectivity, on the other hand, one is drowned in the waters. The resolving third is the losing of the ego in living awareness; of such are the moments and experiences of supreme revelation, beauty, charisma. The supreme identity loses the self and all conscious knowledge of it; nothing remains of either the objective as the thing perceived or the subjective as the perceiver; the subject-object relationship ceases.

As with good and bad, there is no suggestion of preference in the weak and the strong. "Weak" is not used in any pejorative sense. In fact the weak, left, *yin* was always the place of honor in China, since it was the side of nonviolence and thus peace. The right side, the strong, *yang* sword arm, by its very strength, tends to violence and therefore to dissipation and ultimate self-destruction. Only in military matters and in time of war, when violence was the order of the day, did the right side become the position of honor.

One of the outstanding teachings of Taoism is the strength of weakness. The *yin* power of passivity is more enduring than the *yang* force of direct action; the one has a controlled, sustained power, the other is quickly spent and dissipated. This strength-in-weakness is also connected with the symbolism of the valley and the womb. It is that which receives and accepts all things, but from which, in turn, all things emerge. It is because it is the lowest, humblest place that the valley receives the full force of the waters which fall into it from the high, *yang* places. Majestic waterfalls and turbulent mountain torrents, for all their power, come down to the lowly and are absorbed by it and converted into the deep-flowing, broad, quiet and irresistible forces of the rivers, lakes, and oceans, the *yin* principle.

Opposed to the *yin*-water principle is the *yang*-fire, but both these powers are ambivalent as the forces of either destruction or creation. This dual role is also found in Nature herself, who can be ruthlessly destructive or benevolent in giving unstintingly of life, like the Great Mother, of whom Kwan-yin is the Chinese manifestation in her two aspects of creator and destroyer, life and death, holding within herself the tension of opposites which is the process of transformation through Wisdom (*yin*) and Method (*yang*) into the ultimate unity, the Tao. She is both Queen of Heaven and the Great Earth Mother, the Tellus Mater, from whom all things are born and to whom all return. If she can be cruel and ruthless and fearful she is yet "kind and gentle and indulgent, ever a handmaid in the service of mortals, producing under our compulsion, or lavishing of her own accord. What scents and savors, what surfaces for touch, what colors!… What produce she fosters for our benefit!"[10]

If the two forces are working in perfect balance, a unity is achieved which becomes a power in itself and has a controlled force behind it. On the other hand, imbalance and disharmony have no power, but disintegrate into total ineffectiveness. Anything out of harmony, wrong, or maladjusted, either physi-

[10] Pliny, *Natural History*, Book II, LXIII.

Statue of Kwan-yin at the Hsi Hsia temple, Chiang-su province

cally, mentally, or spiritually in the individual in particular, or the world in general, is to be regarded as a failure in, or disturbance of, the balance of the *yin-yang* forces. This applies not only to human beings but to all life in the maintenance of its health and wellbeing. "If the equilibrium of the positive and negative is disturbed ... man himself suffers physically thereby."[11] So in olden days in China, doctors were paid to maintain this balance and were fined if their patients became ill, since this was regarded as a failure on the part of the doctor.

The two great powers at work in the world can be beneficient or hostile according to the

[11] *Chuang Tzu* XXI, trans. Giles.

conduct of the individual or the state in either maintaining or disturbing the equilibrium. When the balance is disrupted the masculine and feminine are in conflict and then they, instead of being creative and harmonious, become malign and destructive, each striving for dominance and thereby producing inflation of the personal ego, developing it out of proportion, and from that arises discord and violence. Neither should usurp the function of the other. Each, in its normal working, corrects the inadequacies or excesses of the other. But the *yin-yang* is not only perfect duality and relationship in manifestation; the whole symbol is also contained within the circle of unity, the Tao, so that the whole is at once the symbol of duality and non-duality. It is the Great Monad and the duality which arises from it. "Existence and non-existence give rise to each other." It is a divine union, the very essence of all spiritual and earthly life. The "Two" arise from the "One" and are inseparable.

On the spiritual plane the *yin* and *yang* are the immanent and transcendent aspects of the Tao, the in-breathing and out-breathing of the Spirit. On the mundane plane, in religion, the active and passive are the two-way traffic of positive outgoing in devotional and ritual worship, and the passive, mystic, receptive ingoing of assimilation back into the One or the Tao, a unity of knowing and being.

As a symbol the diagram of the *yin-yang* is perfection itself. Its symbolism is the acme of simplicity and the whole depth of profundity. It is inexhaustible because it contains all possibilities within itself.

The *Yin-Yang*

4. THE *PA KUA*

The dualism of the *yin-yang* is also expressed by the two lines, the broken — — *yin*, and the unbroken —— *yang*, known as the Two Determinants. These produce the Four Designs, or the *yin* and *yang* in each of their two phases of static and movable, which, in turn, give rise to the Eight Trigrams, known as the *Pa Kua*, that is the manifestations which emerge from the *yin-yang* forces. "The Primeval Pair produce the Four Forms, from which are derived the Eight Trigrams.... The Sages have seen the complexity of the universe. They used these symbols to represent the different forms and to symbolize the different characteristics thereof."[1]

The doctrine of the *yin-yang* principles, their cosmic significance and working in the phenomenal world together with the creative aspect of their interplay and mutations, is contained in the *Yi Ching*, the "Book of Changes", or the "Book of Transformations", a work which was probably re-edited by Confucius but contained a cosmology which was of far greater antiquity than either Taoism or Confucianism, but which was used by, and is basic to, both these philosophies. Legend attributes it to Fu-hsi and it was said to have been added to by King Wu, who declared that "Heaven is the universal Father; Earth the universal Mother", thus introducing the *yin-yang* principle. The ideograph *Yi* is composed of an upper part meaning "sun" and a lower "moon". The "changes" are contained in the mystic diagrams which represent the *yin* and the *yang* in all possible combinations and proportions: these are the Eight Trigrams, since this is the full number which can be made up of the two lines of *yin* and *yang*, symbolizing, as does the *yin-yang* circular figure, the dualistic aspect of nature (which is the "same" and the "other" of Plato) and the entire cosmos and all qualities in it, its primary unity and manifest diversity. "*Yi* has no thought, no action. It is in itself still and calm, yet in its functions it embraces all phenomena and events in the universe."[2]

The trigrams, which are linked symbolically, are doubled to form the hexagrams and symbolize the transformations and transmutations which take place in the realm of becoming and in the separateness brought about by creation and manifestation, as well as the actual unity still existing in apparent diversity and the final attainment of harmony.

The eight trigrams expand to the sixty-four hexagrams, one of which heads each chapter of the *Yi Ching*. Each trigram represents a force in nature and, necessarily partaking of the *yin-yang* principle, is either passive or active. As the world is in a state of flux there is endless interplay, action and reaction, and this is reflected in the whole realm of phenomena and all the antinomies.

The oldest form of the *Pa Kua* is that attributed to Fu-hsi, who places them in pairs of opposites in a circle, the circumference of which symbolizes time and enclosing space.

[1] Confucius, *The Great Appendix to the Yi Ching.*

[2] Ibid.

This may also be arranged as:

K'un	Ken	K'an	Sun	Chen	Li	Tui	Ch'ien
Greater Yin		**Lesser Yang**		**Lesser Yin**		**Greater Yang**	
YIN				**YANG**			

Pa Kua and *Yin-Yang*

Various aspects of the symbolism of the eight trigrams are:

Ch'ien — *Heaven*. Circle. Father. King. Activity. Creative energy. All that is penetrating. Causation. The omnipotent power of the spirit. *Yang*.

K'un — *Earth*. Square. Mother. Queen. Passivity. Receptive and yielding aspect of the creative spirit. The molding of the *prima materia*. Law. Response. Repose. *Yin*.

Tui — *Lake*. Marshland. Watery exhalations. Outward-going intelligence receptive of wisdom. To collect. Clouds. Rain. Absorption. Impregnation. Fertility. Joyfulness. Pleasure. The valley. *Yin*.

Li — *Fire*. Sun. Heat. Lightning. Brightness. Outward-going consciousness. The beautiful. Zeal. Devotion. Penetration. Purification. *Yang*.

Chen — *Thunder*. Quickening energy. Power. Impulse. Arousing. To move. Spring. Growth. *Yang*.

Sun — *Wind*. Mind. Intellect. Penetration. Breath of life. To distribute. Spirit. Wood. *Yang*.

K'an — *Water*. Rivers. The sea. Darkness. Winter. The emotions. The desire nature. Instability. Envelopment. A hollow. Danger. Purification. *Yin*.

☶ Ken — *Mountain*. Physical nature. Separateness. Solitude. To ascend. The immovable. The perverse. *Yang*.

The interdependence of the two great principles and their complex powers is demonstrated by the opposing trigrams of fire and water. Fire ☲, *yang*, masculine, positive, etc., has the *yin* broken line at its center. Water ☵, *yin*, feminine, negative, etc., has the *yang* line enclosed between two *yin*. This also carries the implication of the ambivalence of fire and water which can be both creative and destructive: so can *yin-yang*, at different stages and according to circumstance, be interchangeable. So, also, in the hexagrams, a strong *yang* line may be in a weak *yin* position and vice versa, but these out-of-order situations are symbolically "improper". The hexagrams are, in themselves, an illustration of *yin-yang* since they are made up of two interrelated trigrams. Each succeeding one of the sixty-four hexagrams also follows the *yin-yang* pattern of opposites. For example, creativity is followed by passivity, interaction by conflict, movement by arrest, accomplished by not-yet-accomplished.Again, as with the *yin-yang* circle symbolism, not only are the *yin* and *yang* lines represented in the absolute state, but they, too, can be depicted as moving-relative. They then symbolize movement in the opposite direction, that is to say, towards their own opposites. The moving *yin* is, diagrammatically, — X —, while the moving *yang* is — O —.

From the *yin-yang* interaction springs the whole manifest universe and with it the five elements, or "agents", are produced—fire, water, wood, metal, and earth. These are cosmic forces which, in turn, through their interaction, evolve the phenomenal world of the Ten Thousand Things (the number ten thousand being symbolic of too many to count). The five elements also represent the four cardinal points: fire-south; wood-east; metal-west; water-north, with earth occupying the central position. The four directions in turn control the four seasons, with earth again as the fifth, central, and controlling factor since none of the others has any power unless based on earth.

The cyclic changes of the seasons in the year lead to the cycle of the years. A cycle was sixty years, each having a separate name. Diagrammatically, these were arranged as radii of a circle, enclosing the *yin-yang* symbol and were read from the top, anti-clockwise, thus following the tradition of the left-hand place of honor. This introduces the cyclic view of the cosmos with, as Frithjof Schuon says, "all the primary and secondary phases of affirmation and negation, exteriorization, and introversion, protection and regeneration, that these rhythms comprise."[3]

Taoist cosmology is cyclic, not evolutionary. The world is in a perpetual state of flux and man is in a state of becoming, which is not necessarily a forward movement. The wise man, or Sage, identifies himself with this process of transformation and as he "goes along with creation" he becomes one with the Tao. Man himself is a universe in miniature, being made up physically of the five elements and mentally and spiritually of the *yin* and *kwei* and *yang* and *shan* spirits. As with the macrocosm, so with the microcosm of man. All these parts are in a continual state of flux, of creation and emanation, of dissolution and withdrawal. "Being and non-being grow out of

[3] Frithjof Schuon, *Treasures of Buddhism*.

one another."[4] The *kwei* (often misinterpreted as devils, but which are, in fact, daemons or the superhumans, though they became devils in later, decadent Taoism) are "spirit returning" *yin*, and as such represent the region of death. The *shan* are the "spirit coming", symbolizing both life and *yang*.

For Taoism the soul, the feminine *yin*, wisdom, is the means by which the *yang* intellect attains insight and understanding, together partaking of the *yin-yang* dualistic nature. There is also the *shan*, which is the heavenly part of the *hun*, the spiritual nature which ascends to heaven at the dissolution of the body, and the *kwei* which reverts to the earth element. Together they are known as the *kwei-shan*. Of them Confucius said: "The intelligent spirit is the *shan* nature, the animal soul is the *kwei* nature. It is the union of the *kwei* and the *shan* that forms the highest exhibition of doctrine.... The spirit issues forth and is displayed on high in a condition of glorious brightness."[5] Ch'ang says: "The *kwei-shan* are the energetic operations of Heaven and Earth, and the traces of production and transformation". While Chu Hsi expresses it as: "If we can speak of one breath, then by *shan* is denoted its advancing and developing, and by *kwei* its returning and reverting. If we speak of two breaths, then by *kwei* is denoted the efficaciousness of the secondary or inferior one, and the *shan* by the superior one. They are really only one thing."[6]

When they are spoken of as "demons" the *kwei* merely represent the dark aspect of totality, the irrational, which is why they are feared since the irrational is unpredictable and man generally likes to indulge in the illusion of some sort of security and of knowing where he stands; but in Taoism the *kwei* are accepted and therefore given a normal place and thus robbed of their terrors. In religions where there is an absolute evil, or Devil, this force is immediately turned into a totally hostile power in conflict with both God and man, whereas in Taoism both light and dark have their natural place; or, as Buddhism teaches: "the cause of life is death", the one automatically arising from the other. "Stillness is the end of motion, while evil is the change of good; and good is a kind of life, while evil is a kind of death. It is not that these two opposites are generated together, but they are all one with life."[7]

Since Taoism is cyclic in outlook it naturally does not worship at the shrine of progress. As Emerson says, "Society never advances. It recedes as fast on one side as it gains on the other.... Not in time is the race progressive." Modern history, as an example, has seen the abolition of slavery and child labor together with the torture, murder, and slavery of millions of people and children in the concentration camps of Nazi Germany, Siberia, and modern China. The social conscience is extremely tender on the rights of some children and old people while others die in thousands of malnutrition. Comparatively minute sums are spent on famine relief while hundreds of millions are poured into nuclear powers of destruction and technological *hubris* in outer space. K. S. Sorabji asks, "Progress towards what, from what? It is progress when a fruit from being merely bad, becomes a deliquescent mess—progress in the process of decomposition. The same thing is true of

[4] *Tao Te Ching* II, trans. Waley.

[5] Li Chi, XXI. 2.1. *Record of Rites*. Confucian texts from the last century B.C.

[6] *The Doctrine of the Mean*, trans. Legge.

[7] Jinsai, *Doji-mon*.

'advance', though the fact that the word is often associated with an advanced state of decay may in some small way act as a check upon the fantasies of modern sentimental 'Progressivist' cant."[8] While R. L. Nettleship comments, "Certainly as far as human power of observation goes, it seems idle to talk of permanent 'progress'. We have absolutely no means of judging whether what we call the history of the world is progress or not. Even if we could continuously trace progress for a century, there is nothing to lead us to suppose that it might not cease at any moment and become regress.... We see that progress at one point is generally accompanied by regress in some other."[9] The only real progress that can be made is in inner space, in the attainment of enlightenment which releases from the concepts and bondage of both space and time. The cyclic view of the cosmos applies also to the individual in the universe; there is a perpetual process of ascent and descent, growth and decay, life and death. In the world of relativity all is in movement and everything is perishable and contingent, but beyond this contingency and flux is the immobility of the Absolute, the Tao to which the relative must return. Going out from the One originally into duality and the world of the Ten Thousand Things, man must first find the coincidence of the opposites in unity and so return to his origins and re-establish the original oneness of the Tao. "In the light of the Tao the affirmative and negative are one; the objective becomes one with the subjective.... When subjective and objective are both without their correlates, that is the very axis of Tao, and when the axis passes through the center at which all infinites converge, positive and negative alike blend into an infinite One."[10]

The Tao has also been called "The Supreme Oneness". "Whole, Entire, All, are words which sound differently, but which mean the same. Their purport is One."[11] But the wholeness is no vague theory, no far-off thing; it is a way of life involving everyday life on which the spiritual is based. "Preserve the original One, while resting in harmony with externals." What matters is how one views these externals. "The true man unifies nature and man and equalizes all things. To him there is no mutual opposition in all things. There is no mutual conquest of nature and man."[12] "To see all things in the yet undifferentiated, primordial unity, or from such a distance that all melts into one, this is true intelligence."[13] Plotinus teaches the same doctrine when he says, "Now the Supreme, because within it there are no differences, is eternally present, but we achieve such presence only when our differences are lost."[14]

All Taoist writings and allegories emphasize the oneness of all creation; mankind and all things that live are fragmentary manifestations of the whole. In the world of appearances they seem to lead a separate existence, but this is illusory, in reality they are limbs, or organs, of one body, just as each apparently separate body is made up of various parts. In the perfect, primordial state there was mutual fellowship between all things. Traditionally,

[8] K. S. Sorabji, "The Validity of the Aristocratic Principle" from *Art and Thought*.

[9] R.L. Nettleship, *The Philosophical Remains of R.L. Nettleship* (ed. A.C. Bradley, published by Macmillan, second edition 1901).

[10] *Chuang Tzu* II, trans. Fung Yu-lan.

[11] *Chuang Tzu* XXII, trans. Giles.

[12] Kuo Hsiang, *Commentaries on Chuang Tzu*, trans. Fung Yu-lan.

[13] Lao Tzu.

[14] *Enneads* VI, IX, 8, trans. Dodds.

Ma Yüan (active c. 1190-after 1225), *Gazing at Spring Mountains*, Southern Sung dynasty

this obtained in early times in the Golden Age when man and animals spoke the same language. It is a mark of the Sage that he can recapture this state and communicate naturally with all living things. The more integrated a person the less separate he is (that is not to say "gregarious", but that he feels himself at one with life) and the more he realizes the interdependence and interpenetration of all life. The most separate person is the totally isolated and lonely psychotic. The separatist moves towards and stays on the circumference of the circle, for ever wandering round in the same circuit. Any movement away from the center takes one further into the world of manifestation, the multiplicity and diffusion of the Ten Thousand Things. This is Lao Tzu's meaning in saying "The further one travels the less one knows". It is the journey back to the center which starts and completes the process of integration. The circumference is the restricted, literally circumscribed, view of life, but from the center it is possible to see in all directions with the minimum of effort and movement. The center is the ultimate simplicity. As René Guénon puts it: "At the central point all oppositions inherent in more external points of view are transcended, all oppositions have disappeared and are resolved in a perfect equilibrium … the neutral point at the center at which there can be no conflicts." It is also the center of power, the quintessence of the alchemists which is "the reassembly of his powers" and "the concentration of his nature". It is Aristotle's Motionless Mover; a "unity without dimensions" and it is to "return to one's roots". It is the point containing the Will of Heaven, the Wholeness, the Tao.

Chuang Tzu says, "it is the glory of man to know that all things are One and that life and death are but phases of the same existence." "Life follows death. Death is the beginning of Life. Who knows when the end is reached?… If, then, life and death are but consecutive states, what need have I to complain? All things are One. What we love is animation, what we hate is corruption; but corruption in its turn becomes animation, and animation once more becomes corruption."[15] In another place he writes, "Only the truly intelligent know the unity of things. They therefore do not make distinctions, but follow the common and the ordinary. The common and the ordinary are the natural function of all things, which express the common nature of the whole. Following the common nature of the whole, they are happy. Being happy, they are near to perfection."[16]

The fall from the primordial perfection is, for the Taoist, the making of distinctions, the bringing about of separateness. "The knowledge of the ancients was perfect. How perfect? At first they did not know there were things. This is the most perfect knowledge: nothing can be added. Next they knew there were things, but did not yet make distinctions between them. Next they made distinctions between them, but they did not yet pass judgments upon them. When judgments were passed, Tao was destroyed. With the destruction of Tao, individual preferences came into being."[17] But Chuang Tzu, the Sage, returning to primordial perfection and realizing the Supreme Unity could say, "The Universe and I came into being together, and I, and everything therein, are One."

Yin-Yang and the Eight Trigrams

[15] *Chuang Tzu* XII, trans. Giles.

[16] *Chuang Tzu* II, trans. Fung Yu-lan.

[17] Ibid.

左第五十三

5. CHUANG TZU & THE SAGES

In Chuang Tzu's writings it is difficult to know where philosophy ends and poetry begins, he is the poet-philosopher and metaphysical poet. In him, the philosophical reasoning faculty and poetic intuition are admirably combined. "Brilliant", "sparkling", "pithy", are words which every commentator is forced to use of Chuang Tzu. In his works the brevity of the *Tao Te Ching* is expanded and the concise, epigrammatic sayings of Lao Tzu are developed and enriched with "exquisite parables and pungent aphorisms".[1] He writes with a terse brilliancy of style, but while Lao Tzu is compact to the point of the adamantine, Chuang Tzu writes with a resilient fluency and flexibility, with gaiety, immense verve, and a degree of puckishness. Lao Tzu is original, epigrammatic, and wholly detached, with no attempt at teaching: Chuang Tzu's flowing style is, by contrast, persuasive, attractive, and instructive. Both are compelling in their separate ways.

In view of the uncertain origin of the *Tao Te Ching*, it is of great value to have Lao Tzu's famous disciple to expand and interpret the teaching of his master. In Chuang Tzu we have the luxuriant flowering of Taoism and his works not only display all the refinement and beauty of Chinese art, but also have the salty tang of criticism combined with a degree of skepticism added to mysticism. As Lao Tzu joined issue with the sophistication and artificiality of his time, so later the greatest follower and exponent of his doctrines rose to campaign against the excessive conventionalism and ceremonialism which Confucius had left imprinted on Chinese public and family life, and in his writings much of this criticism of the sobriety and conventional rigidity of Confucianism was put into humorous and apocryphal meetings between Lao Tzu and Confucius which are used as parables by Chuang Tzu so that the widely differing teachings of the two could be contrasted. It was typical of the Taoist Sage to combine humor with profound thought. No other metaphysical treatises have been written with such verve and underlying laughter.

The Book of Chuang Tzu is divided into three parts, the Inner Chapters (I-VII), the Outer (VIII-XXII), and the Miscellaneous (XXIII-XXXIII), and just as the works attributed to Lao Tzu and Lieh Tzu show the hand of a commentator and redactor, so parts of *Chuang Tzu* are obviously interpolated and show a superficiality of thought and lack of order in argument that could have nothing to do with the depth and lucidity of Chuang Tzu's brilliant mind. Even so, the interpolations are the words of scholars; anyone able to write on the classics was *ipso facto* a scholar. There was, in China, no such thing as the semi-illiterate scribe who copied manuscripts mechanically and, through his ignorance, often misinterpreted and muddled the sense. The copying of the ancient Chinese classics was done by people who not only understood the material on which they worked, but who could, and usually did, add their own com-

[1] K. Saunders. *A Pageant of Asia* (published by Oxford University Press, 1934).

Opposite: *Former Taoist Sages*, Ming dynasty, c. 1460, Pao Ning Temple, Shan Hsi Province ments. Thus, very few texts were likely to survive in their original form or to express the unalloyed opinions of their supposed authors. Some of these comments and passages were inserted with skill and are difficult to detect, but most of them are obvious. As the Chinese saying goes—"A sable robe cannot be patched with dogs' tails".

In his inimitable style, Oscar Wilde writes, "Chuang Tzu, whose name must carefully be pronounced as it is *not* written, is a very dangerous writer, and a publication of his book in English, two thousand years after his death, is obviously premature, and may cause a great deal of pain to many thoroughly respectable and industrious people. It may be true that the ideal of self-culture and self-development, which is the aim of his scheme of philosophy, is an ideal somewhat needed in an age like ours, in which most people are so anxious to educate their neighbors, that they have actually no time left in which to educate themselves. But would it be wise to say so? It seems to me that if once we admitted the force of any one of Chuang Tzu's destructive criticisms we should have to put some check in our national habit of self-glorification, and the only thing that ever consoles man for the stupid things he does is the praise he always gives himself for doing them."[2]

Chuang Tzu was offered, and refused, the high office of Prime Minister of the State of Chu, preferring the liberty of the natural life of the sage to the restricted artificiality of the city. The incident is told with characteristic, humorous brevity. The Sage was fishing one day when an imperial deputation arrived to offer him the position of Prime Minister. Without looking up he said, "I hear that there is a sacred tortoise which your Prince keeps in a chest in his ancestral shrine, though it has been dead these three thousand years. Do you suppose it would prefer to be venerated in death, or to be alive and wagging its tail in the mud?" "Surely the latter", said the officials. "Then away with you", said the philosopher, "and leave me to wag mine!"

It was in the works of Chuang Tzu that Taoism developed its essentially mystical character to the full. To attain understanding it is necessary to go directly to the nature of things themselves, reason and argument cannot supply the answer. "Suppose that you argue with me. If you beat me instead of my beating you, are you necessarily right? Is one of us right and the other wrong, or both of us right and both of us wrong? Both of us cannot come to a mutual understanding, and

Lu Tung Pin Receiving the Secrets of Taoism from Chung-li Ch'üan, anonymous, Yüan dynasty, 14th century

[2] Oscar Wilde in *The Speaker*.

others are all in the dark. Whom shall I ask to decide this dispute? I may ask someone who agrees with you: but since he agrees with you, how can he decide it? I may ask someone who agrees with me, but since he agrees with me, how can he decide it? I may ask someone who differs from both you and me, but since he differs from both you and me, how can he decide it? In this way you and I and all others would not be able to come to a mutual and common understanding: shall we wait for still another?"[3]

The answer of mysticism is that one must penetrate into "the realm of the Infinite and take refuge therein". "The Sages embrace all things, while men in general argue about them in order to convince each other. Great Tao does not admit of being spoken … speech that argues falls short of its aim." "Tao has no distinctions. Speech cannot be applied to the eternal.… What is beyond this world the sages do not discuss, although they do not deny its existence. What is within this world the sages discuss, but do not pass judgments."[4]

This entering into the realm of the Infinite is also a return to the center and away from the idea of separateness, to lose the seeming self in the One. In Taoist phraseology it is to find one's true nature, or in Buddhist terms, to be what one is. There are not two selves, only one Self or Reality. The other so-called self, the ego, belongs entirely to the phenomenal world and disappears like a reflected light when the great source of all light is recognized. As Sri Ramana Maharshi says, there cannot be two selves since man does not have a self, he *is* it, the Real Self. There is no point in looking for what one already is. The work of Taoism is, as in all mysticism, to make man realize he is this true Self, the Tao, and to unite him with it again.

The term "mysticism" is often greatly misunderstood and confused with some woolly-minded and amorphous feeling, or an orgy of religious emotionalism, or psychic experiences to be found in trance or even synthetically in drugs. Mysticism may be inexpressible, but there is nothing nebulous about it. Least of all is it daydreaming, which is the ultimate descent into the world of the Ten Thousand Things, a playing with shadows of shadows. The real mysticism requires as difficult a spiritual exercise as man can undertake. "The truly great man ignores self: this is the height of self discipline."[5] It is the discarding of the self of separateness, of prejudice, and of opinions. Opinions are based on sensory knowledge which is an ever-shifting sand, fragmentary and partial, changing with individuals, with experience, with ethnic groups and in different ages. Opinion gives substance to the impermanent and makes entities out of evanescence. Only immediate knowledge is valid, the direct apprehending of the thing-in-itself, the whole, the breakthrough to the meaning behind appearance.

According to Fichte, mysticism is "far sight". This is true of its out-going powers in reaching for the transcendent, but it is equally "near sight" in an immanent sense, teaching man the nature of his innermost Being.

Taoism knows nothing of the emotional expressions of mysticism in the West, there are in it none of the agonies of abasement, no miseries, no erotic symbolisms and hysterical extremes of feeling brought about by ascetic exercises and maltreating the physical body.

[3] *Chuang Tzu* II, trans. Fung Yu-lan.

[4] Ibid.

[5] *Chuang Tzu* XVII, trans. Giles.

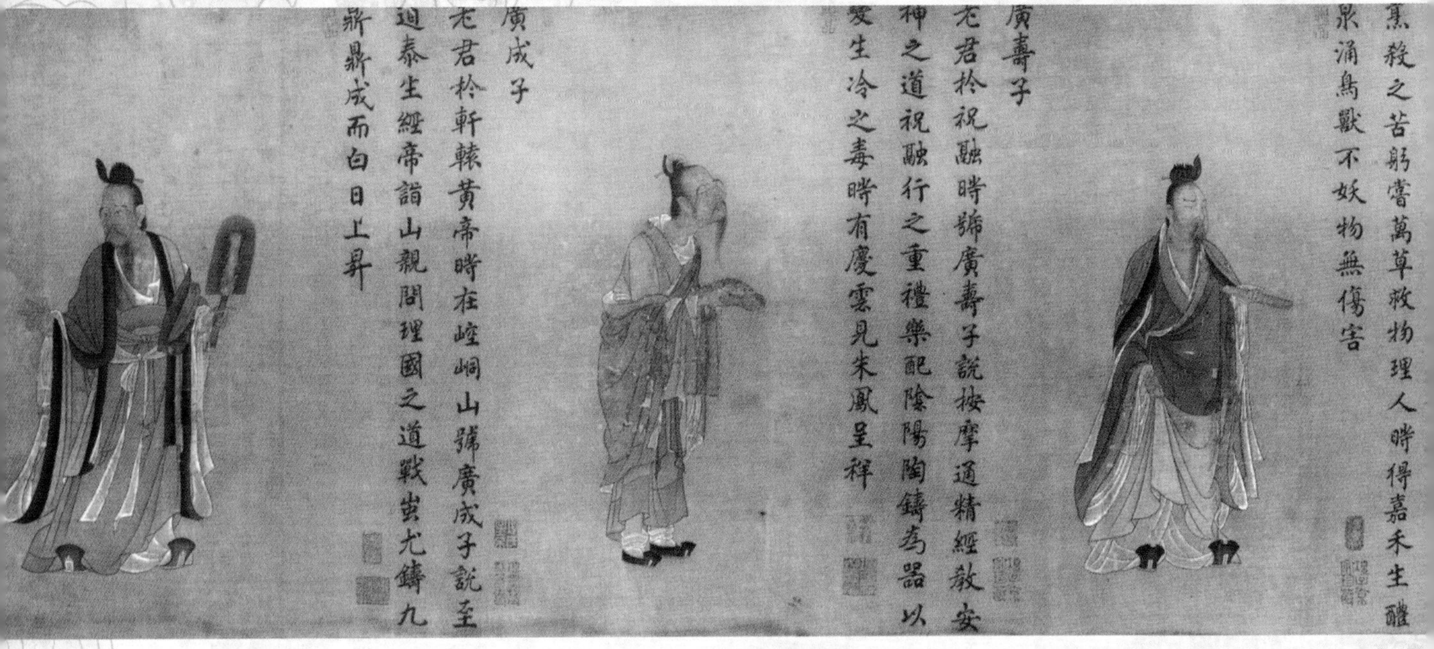

Wang Li Yung (active 1120-after 1145), *The Transformations of Lord Lao*, Southern Sung dynasty, early 12th century

This, to Taoism, is a violation of nature. The body, as much as the soul, has its right as an instrument and must be kept in balance and harmony, both are good servants of the spirit and no one wants an ill-treated and crippled servant. Nor is there any need to regard the body as a prison-house of the soul, but merely as a house, with all its limiting attributes, but also with its doors and windows. It is in occupation for a time and is useful for that time and needs to be kept in due order. The ascetic keeps a hovel of a dwelling; the sensualist is like a house-proud woman whose house possesses her rather than she possessing it. The only prison-house is of man's own building of the hard blocks of rigid ideas, prejudices, forms, and names. Austerities and indulgences are equally an imbalance and a disturbance of the *yin-yang* harmony. Taoist mysticism is an intellectual, not an emotional, exercise; it has no personal God by whom it can feel accepted or rejected. Instead there is a calm contemplation of the sublime immensity of the universe and an entering into the smallest detail of nature. "Tao is not too small for the greatest, nor too great for the smallest. Thus all things are embraced therein: wide indeed is its boundless capacity, unfathomable its depth."[6]

Eastern mysticism is like a snowy peak towering into the clouds, often hidden from view, and certainly the summit can never be seen from the base. Only trained climbers are fit to tackle its rigors and perils. Western philosophy, on the other hand, is like a plain over which anyone can caper at will, in any direction, largely getting nowhere and crossing and recrossing the same trails. In the East philosophy is regarded as useless if it has no effect on character. Its whole point is to produce the Perfect Man, the Sage. The brain-without-character type, the dry-as-dust academic, and the absent-minded professor are regarded as

[6] Ibid., XIII.

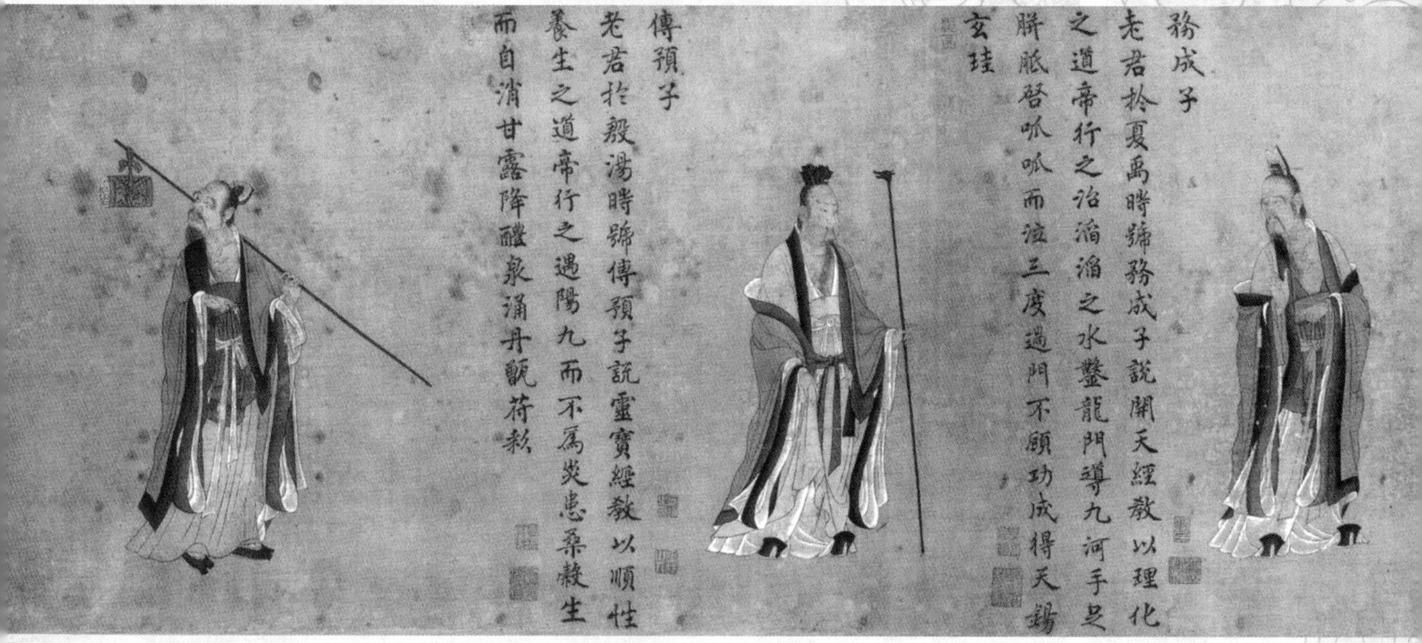

unbalanced and therefore as failures. Wholeness is required of the Sage, he is the quintessence of human possibilities, in whom all potentialities are realized. Although it may have its head in the clouds, Taoism has its feet firmly on the earth. Of Chuang Tzu, as an example, it was said, "Chuang Tzu moves in the realms below while soaring to Heaven above",[7] and "in paradoxes, in daring words, with profound subtlety he let his imagination soar.… Above he roams in the company of Heaven, below he is the companion of such as are beyond life and death, and deny the reality of beginning and end."[8]

To be "beyond life and death" is the mark of the Sage, the man who is variously described as the Perfect Man, the True Man, one who has attained "The Great Whole", although the term is occasionally used in the sense of a man of knowledge, but it is never to be confused with the saint. A saint can be made in a matter of seconds through the process known as conversion. The Sage is the result of the gradual withdrawal from the illusions of the sense into the reality of the Tao, of the attainment of wisdom, of enlightenment, of a profound gnosis which, too, is "beyond life and death" and implies a complete acceptance of all things as they are. "He who clearly apprehends the scheme of existence does not rejoice over life, nor repine at death; for he knows that terms are not final."[9] "His glory is to know that all things are One and that life and death are but phases of the same existence."[10] "The True Man of old knew neither love of life nor fear of death. Living, he felt no elation, dying, he offered no resistance. Unconsciously he went, unconsciously he

[7] Ibid., XVII.

[8] *Chuang Tzu* XXXIII, trans. Saunders.

[9] *Chuang Tzu* XVII, trans. Giles.

[10] Ibid., XII.

came; that was all.... He received with delight anything that came to him.... Being such his mind was free.... He was in harmony with all things."[11] "When we come it is because we have the occasion to be born. When we go we simply follow the natural course. Those who are quiet at the proper occasion and follow the course of nature cannot be affected by sorrow and joy. These men were considered by the ancients as people who were released from bondage."[12] For the Sage "there is a change of lodging, but no real death". "The Universe carries me in my body, toils me through my life, gives me repose in old age, and rests me in death. What makes my life good makes my death good also."[13]

The Sage is "he who has entered the state of repose". He has passed from the moving circumference of the cosmic wheel to its immovable center. This also represents the utter simplicity of the Sage as opposed to the considerable but transient volume of worldly knowledge of the ordinary scholar. The perfect man moves the wheel by the mere fact of his presence and without involving himself or concerning himself with the exertion of any effort. "The absolutely simple man sways all beings by his simplicity ... so that nothing opposes him.... Opposing nothing, he can be opposed by nothing.... Fire and water cannot harm him."[14] He is the man who has actualized his potential and holds the *yin* and *yang* in perfect balance, in which action and potentiality are fully and equally realized and Heaven and Earth are at One. Though still having to act, he is not involved in action and abstains from any desires as to the results of such action. "Such a man will leave gold in the hillside and pearls in the sea. He will not struggle for wealth, nor strive for fame. He will not rejoice at old age, nor grieve over early death. He will find no pleasure in success, no chagrin in failure."[15]

The simplicity of the wise man implies a reasonable outlook on life: he is unsophisticated, unconfused, uncorrupted by the sophistry of the so-called intelligentsia who are, as a rule, more concerned with their own image as intelligentsia and more taken up with the desire to impress and be appreciated, than with basic realities. It is no mere accident, but a serious symptom of the disease of the times that words such as "sophistication" change status, and that which means "adulterated", "impure", "not genuine" should become a term of approbation and commendation, just as luxuries and trivialities are multiplied and converted into supposed necessities, which is also a symptom of decadence. These trends are followed by licence and a general dulling of the social conscience which, in turn, leads to the callousness and cruelty of societies satiated with luxuries on the one side and starving on the other.

Simplicity is no theoretical expediency: it is the key to happiness because it is a state of desirelessness. It does away with the "condition of chronic desire, which cannot be allayed by attaining its ostensible object, because that object is not the cause but the excuse".[16] Desire, grasping, coveting, all destroy the life they feed upon. One of Chuang Tzu's telling allegories deals with this. "The ruler of the Southern Sea is called Change; the ruler of the North-

[11] *Chuang Tzu* VI, trans. Fung Yu-lan.

[12] Ibid.

[13] Ibid.

[14] "Fire" and "water" symbolize the contraries of the phenomenal world.

[15] *Chuang Tzu* XII, trans. Giles.

[16] A. M. Hocart, *The Life-giving Myth* (ed. Lord Raglan, published by Methuen, 1970).

Ma Yüan, *Scholars Conversing Beneath Blossoming Plum Trees*, Southern Sung dynasty

ern Sea is called Uncertainty, and the ruler of the Center is called Primitivity.[17] Change and Uncertainty often met on the territory of Primitivity and, being well treated by him, determined to repay his kindness. They said, 'All men have seven holes for seeing, hearing, eating, and breathing. Primivity alone has none of these. Let us try to bore some for him.' So every day they bored one hole; but on the seventh day Primitivity died."[18]

The full significance of simplicity, however, is not the attainment of temporal happiness and a certain character, although it fol-

[17] The "primitive" in the Taoist sense is the man of wisdom and genius; he is what he is, quite naturally and inexplicably.

[18] *Chuang Tzu* VI, trans. Fung Yu-lan.

The Immortal Chung-li Ch'üan, attributed to Chao Ch'i, Ming dynasty, late 15th century

lows that in a state of simplicity man would be content. Not possessing more than he needed, he would not himself be possessed. Crime would not exist since, without desires and envying others' possessions the incentive to most crime goes. "Make excursion in pure simplicity. Identify yourself with non-distinction. Follow the nature of things and admit no personal bias, then the world will be at peace."[19] Simplicity is also the return to the undifferentiated center, the ultimate simplicity of the dimensionless point; the condition of wholeness.

An old Chinese story, intended to illustrate destiny, was adapted by Chuang Tzu to give an example of the folly of desire and the fact that "loss follows the pursuit of gain". A man stood watching and speculating on a cicada happily sunning itself on a summer day, unaware of a praying mantis poised ready to pounce on it. A bird seized the mantis, while the man drew his bow to shoot the bird, himself unaware that he was being stalked by a tiger, ready to spring.

To correct the folly of ambition, Taoism takes a puckish delight in pointing out the value of uselessness: the magnificent, but crooked, tree which has attained full growth because it is useless to the carpenter; the cripple who is not conscripted but also gets extra rations out of pity for his condition. Chuang Tzu laughs at the man who seeks fame, position, or glory and says that the perfect man would regard these as being "handcuffs and fetters", and that "he who acts for fame, and thus loses his own nature, is not a man of learning".[20]

Simplicity requires a total acceptance of life, a quality which is not to be confused with tolerance with all its overtones of condescension and superiority of judgment, but a complete understanding and entering into. Nor is it resignation, usually tinged with self-pity, but an absolute acceptance which seeks to find the inner meaning of all experience and the attainment of discernment and wisdom in liv-

[19] Ibid.
[20] Ibid.

ing. "Among men, reject none, among things reject nothing. This is called comprehensive intelligence." It is also the release from fear and apprehension which are merely man-made imaginations of things which might occur. The Sage is "happy under prosperous and adverse circumstances alike.... Nothing can harm him"[21] ... "he takes things as they come and is not overwhelmed."[22]

With simplicity and acceptance goes spontaneity. The Sage acts with complete simplicity and therefore all his actions are spontaneous, as all perfect action must be. All supreme achievements are effortless; striving belongs to grades before perfection is attained. The perfect man responds "spontaneously, as if there were no choice".[23] "Without knowing how, the great artists spontaneously became artists ... without knowing how, the sages spontaneously became sages. Not only are the sages and artists difficult to imitate, we cannot even be fools, or dogs, by simply wishing or trying to be."[24] Even in relatively good performances, preference goes to the more spontaneous, which is thus regarded as nearer perfection.

Of two young thoro'breds galloping neck
to neck
I'd choose the colt that with least effort held
his course.
Of two runners abreast my liking would
crown him
Who had the greater grace of limb and
show'd no trouble of face.[25]

[21] *Chuang Tzu* XVII, trans. Giles.
[22] Ibid., XXV.
[23] *Chuang Tzu* VI, trans. Fung Yu-lan.
[24] Kuo Hsiang, *Commentaries on Chuang Tzu*.
[25] Robert Bridges, *The Testament of Beauty* IV (published by Clarendon Press, Oxford).

Spontaneity has also the quality of the Tao in that it is what it is. "We may claim that we know the causes of certain things. But there is still a question: what is the cause of these causes? If we continue to ask this question again and again, we have to stop at something that is spontaneously self-produced and is what it is. We cannot ask about the cause of this something. We can only say that it is."[26]

In a metaphysic based on spontaneity it is useless to look for logic, consistency, or any "school of philosophy". Logic is a bull-at-a-gate approach, a direct line of attack. The non-logical approach allows for a change of direction (if you can step aside from a charging bull he will go blindly on and crash on the gate, but you are saved by being able to move sideways), and for taking different ways, so that the object may be seen from all angles. There are few straight lines in nature. Nor is there any need for the sharp either/or outlook, so prevalent in the West, which belongs to the realm of facts, ethics, and mechanics, but not to mysticism. In life one thing can rise from another and the two can easily change places. When the rigid either/or is adopted, each strengthens the other by opposition and conflict and so widens the rift. Hence the small appeal of logic in Eastern thought. Logic is too static and hidebound and often assumes conditions which do not necessarily exist outside the mind of the logician, just as man can make a set of rules, insist on living by them, and then come to believe that they are inexorable. The Eastern mind has never demanded the precision of terms so dear to the scientifically-minded West which likes to have everything neatly labeled and confined behind the rigid bars of a mental prison. This does very

[26] Kuo Hsiang, *Commentaries*.

well for exact science, but is not sufficiently fluid for life, where a wider range of possibilities and latitude of interpretation is needed. Okakura Kakuzo writes of "that broad expanse of love for the ultimate or universal which is the common thought-inheritance of every Asiatic race, enabling them to produce all the great religions of the world, and distinguishing them from those maritime peoples of the Mediterranean and Baltic, who love to dwell on the Particular, and to search out the means, not the end of life". The mists which drift across the Taoist landscapes, the mountain tops disappearing in the clouds, are symbolic of the perpetual flux in the universe and the unnaturalness of the rigid and the fixed. So much is hidden in the mists, so much is impossible of precise knowledge or proof, but that which conceals can also reveal:

> Those shaken mists a space unsettle then
> Round the half-glimpsed turrets slowly wash again;
> But not ere … I first have seen.[27]

The challenge of Taoism to the rational mind finds expression in paradox, the function of which is to jolt the mind out of its logical ruts. The contrary, and even the absurd, reveals a region of knowledge hidden from the pragmatic and sensory world. Taoist writers are experts in *reductio ad absurdum.* Paradox must be accepted in any form of mysticism and Taoism not only uses it but is itself a paradox since it is at one and the same time the most intellectual and the simplest of all ways. It has the wisdom of the child in it and is more in touch with the natural than is reason. It is wholly mystical but insists that "ordinary life is the very Tao". The use of paradox avoids commitments to doctrines and statements which can so easily be systemized, misunderstood, and so rendered sterile. It is not a contradiction in essence, but rather two aspects of one whole. "Tao causes fullness and emptiness, but is not either. It causes renovation and decay, but is not either. It causes beginning and end, but is not either. It causes accumulation and dispersion, but is not either …. Tao makes things what they are, but is not in itself a thing. Nothing can produce Tao; yet everything has Tao within it."[28] Paradoxically, Tao does nothing but accomplishes all things. Formless itself, it is the origin of all forms; it is unchanging, yet it is diffused everywhere in the world of change. "To seek after Tao is like turning round in circles to see one's own eyes. Those who understand this will walk on."[29] It is the eternal paradox of the Nothing and the All.

Liu Chün, *Immortals Dancing with a Toad* (detail), Ming dynasty, 15th century

[27] Francis Thompson, "The Hound of Heaven".

[28] *Chuang Tzu* XXII, trans. Giles.

[29] From a Taoist Notebook.

6. *WU-WEI*

Wu-wei is another term which defies exact translation so is usually left as it is. It is the doctrine of inaction or non-action, but only a superficial outlook interprets it as *laissez faire*, in the sense of indifference, for the Taoist is not indifferent, but should be totally committed to life. If any translation should be attempted, possibly "non-interference" or "letting-go" is the best. At the lowest level it is a policy of naturalness, of "live and let live" and of avoiding friction, with its inevitable consequences of discord and conflict, whether on the individual or national scale, and allowing the maximum of individual liberty and understanding the views of others. It is also a letting-go, a giving-way, a yielding, primarily a yielding of the self, the ego, as that which is responsible for introducing selfishness and dissonance. At a higher level it is the desirelessness, the dispassionateness, which leads automatically to release from tensions and helps towards realization. Action is normally the outcome of the incessant, and usually feverish, working of the mind taken up with desires, daydreams, and the unproductive turning over of problems which, like desires, are "self" created and self-centered. Problems are solved (which, literally, means "loosened") when tensions are eased and one is able to understand the true nature of a thing, hence "sleeping on it", or the sudden flash of intuition which comes when the rational mind ceases its activity and a spontaneous recognition of reality occurs.

It is a doctrine of immediacy, or, as Chuang Tzu calls it, "non-angularity", of spontaneous adaptation and response and of perfect acceptance; an action which is so unforced and natural that it loses the ordinary meaning of action with its accompanying deliberation and weighing up, and is so in harmony with the natural that it simply *is*, without having to think about it. There is no ulterior motive, indeed, there is no motive at all in such "actionless action", since this activity

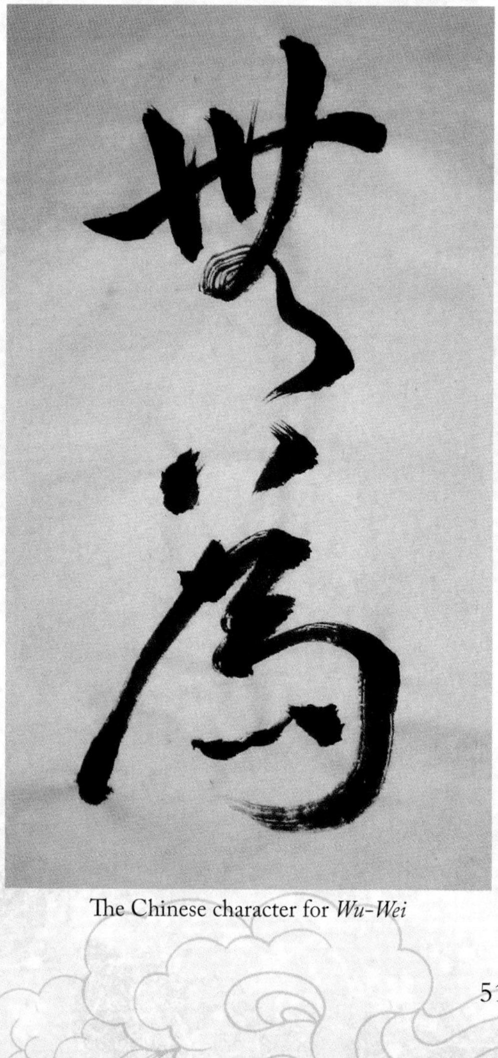
The Chinese character for *Wu-Wei*

is "pivoted on the center of rest" and "requires only such movement as is in accord with the motions of Heaven". The only action necessary is to be in accord with the Tao.

All perfect movement is spontaneous, and as the universe exists effortlessly, so must man. Until he has achieved spontaneity his actions are the result of the will or the deliberations of the rational mind and therefore are artificial and strained and out of harmony with the "motions of Heaven". Movement should be an unfolding, not an exertion; it should be involuntary. This is not to advocate inertness or lethargy. The Sage, although having "knowledge outside the sphere of things", yet "at no time, fails to deal with things. Although his spirit is beyond, yet it is all the time in the world."[1] It is the quiet acceptance of life in the world as it comes and as it is, waiting for the time and season, never forcing an issue, but allowing it to unfold in its own good time and nature. Nor is this a spineless fatalism or pious resignation since it is more than mere acquiescence. It is, in fact, almost gay and is certainly humorous delight in all that life has to offer. In the words of Chuang Tzu, it is to be like sages who "cheerfully played their allotted parts". Actionlessness is an inward quality; it may be passive, but it is a creative passivity. "From inaction comes potentiality of action."

It is senseless to dissipate energy in action for action's sake, in an endless and unproductive agitation. Action should be confined to suitable circumstances. "For traveling by water there is nothing like a boat … this is because a boat moves readily on water; but were you to try to push it on land you would never succeed in making it go", but would have "great trouble and no result except a certain injury to yourself".[2] This "injury to oneself" can also mean injury to others if one urges them also to unsuitable action, or if one indulges in action which is interference and the outcome of outward action arising from the overweening presumption that one knows what is good for others before having achieved goodness oneself. This is shown in the folly of proselytizing and sudden conversion, which do violence to and upset the natural order of development in both nations and people. It involves the extraordinary assumption that one can teach more than one knows, that one can demonstrate a perfection one does not possess. "Act within the limits of your nature, but have nothing to do with what is beyond it. This is the most easy matter of non-action."[3] Man can, of himself, only bring forth that which is in him: from a chaotic, disintegrated mind and character only chaos can emerge. Only through contact with that which is greater than the personal self, by attachment to it and learning from it, can the more-than-human power be attained. The only effective preaching is what one is. When in trouble or distress, to whom will the distressed turn, the man of action or the man of being? Does one consider what the adviser has achieved by way of good works, what he preaches, or what he is himself?

The letting-go of *wu-wei* is also the abandonment of the worship of the false gods of security. The world's sages have all taught the stupidity of the quest for security. Life is dynamic, supple, ever-changing; death is rigid and static. Preoccupation with the morrow, whose problems may never come, lets the present slip by unlived. Paradoxically, the very

[1] *The Discussion on Pan Jo*, trans. Fung Yu-lan.

[2] *Chuang Tzu* XIV, trans. Giles.

[3] Kuo Hsiang, *Commentaries*.

abandonment of the desire for security, the spiritual poverty of no-thing-ness, in the return to the motionless center, is the only security that ever did, or could, exist.

Metaphysically, *wu-wei* is the "actionless activity", the central point of the wheel of life, the potential, the point at which being and knowing become one. It is also the Supreme Identity, since absolute knowledge must imply absolute identity and the Motionless Mover, the Tao that "never acts yet through it all things are done".[4] *Wu-wei* is not the end of all action but the cessation of motivated action. It must not be mistaken for the impassive Stoic *apatheia*, or apathy, based on despair of this world, the almost complete suppression of feelings. It is rather the end of action induced by desires and attachment to the realm of the illusions of the senses. The Stoic worship of reason, to the exclusion of feeling, was too rigid and life-denying and led to an imbalance which has nothing in common with the full acceptance and understanding and the perfect harmony which is the aim of Taoism.

Non-activity is a thing of the mind and spirit, the open mind and pure spirit which can move spontaneously in any direction in any given situation. Humanity is now so highly conditioned in mind by its beliefs and ideologies and worship of factual knowledge, that spontaneity is almost lost. "While there should be no action, there should also be no inaction";[5] that is to say, there should be no deliberate adoption of a line of inaction, which would at once turn it into action. There should be no attachment to inaction any more than action. As the *Bhagavad Gita* says, "Let not the fruits of action be thy motive; neither let there be any attachment to inaction."[6] Both action and inaction are in the realm of duality and, like all opposites, must ultimately be resolved by the return to the motionless center. Kuo Hsiang says, in his *Commentaries on Chuang Tzu*, "Non-action does not mean doing nothing. Let everything do what it really does, and then its nature will be satisfied. Hearing the theory of non-action, some people think that lying is better than walking. These people go too far and misunderstand Chuang Tzu's philosophy."

Lin Yu-tang calls this letting-go "non-assertion", "equilibrium", or even "sitting loose to life". "It is the secret of mastering circumstances without asserting oneself against them; it is the principle of yielding to an oncoming force in such a way as it is unable to harm you. Thus the skilled master of life never opposes things.... He changes them by acceptance, by taking them into his confidence, never by flat denial.... He accepts everything until, by including all things, he becomes their master."[7] This acceptance, and with it receptivity and spontaneity, is basic to Taoism. "One pure act of acceptance is worth more than a hundred thousand exercises of one's will", since it is "a state of interior silence and quietude from which, at the right time, the right action emerges without any volition".[8] Will is the basis of most Western thought, hence the preference for action. "I intend to do this; I want to do that", which ignores the possibility that it might be better to do nothing at all about that particular situation, but to let it develop naturally without gratuitous interference. "The true man of old did not oppose....

[4] *Tao Te Ching* XXXVII, trans. Waley.

[5] *Chuang Tzu* XI, trans. Giles.

[6] *Bhagavad Gita* II, 47.

[7] Lin Yu-tang, *The Importance of Living*.

[8] Fung Yu-lan, *The Spirit of Chinese Philosophy* (published by Routledge & Kegan Paul).

Ch'iao Chung-ch'ang (active 12th century), *The Red Cliff*, c. 1123

He did not seek for heroic accomplishments. He laid no plans. Therefore, he had neither regret in failure nor self-complacency in success. Thus he could scale heights without fear."[9] Attaining the spontaneity of the Tao, actions are motiveless and so do not result in any reaction. "In tranquility, in stillness, in the unconditioned, in inaction, we find the levels of the universe, the very constitution of Tao."[10]

Wu-wei requires daring letting-go. The average person prefers the seeming safety of the logical world with everything neatly labeled and pigeon-holed, so that nothing unexpected or upsetting can occur and one will not be confronted with the unusual, requiring adaptations. This attitude is static and dams up the source of all wisdom, the wonder of the open mind. "The Sage lives in the realm of change and utility and yet abides in the sphere of *wu-wei*; it is within the walls of the nameable and yet out in the open country of what goes beyond speech. He, being silent and alone, empty and all open, his state cannot be clothed in language."[11]

Obviously a corollary of *wu-wei* is non-resistance and non-violence. Lao Tzu advocated not only non-resistance but requiting evil with good, while any form of violence was rightly regarded as the hallmark of the barbarian, or the criminal. "Show me a violent man who has come to a good end and I will take him for my teacher."[12] Violence is an immature and infantile reaction and impossible to a person of culture and maturity. It is always symptomatic of a loss of control and marks the end

[9] *Chuang Tzu* VI, trans. Fung Yu-lan.

[10] *Chuang Tzu* XV, trans. Giles.

[11] Sheng Chao's reply to Lin Yi-min, trans. Fung Yu-lan.

[12] *Tao Te Ching* XLII, trans. Waley.

of human dignity and respect, whether it be an overt act of aggression, destruction, stealing, or a burst of anger or an impatient word or thought, all arising from violence of either body or mind. It also exhausts itself quickly and has no sustained power. "A battering ram can break down a wall, but it cannot repair the breach."[13] "A violent wind cannot last the whole day; pelting rain cannot last the whole morning."[14] Until recent times in China the first man to strike a blow in a quarrel was held to be the loser, just as it was said that the bravest man draws his weapon last. In such a climate of thought war was regarded, naturally, as inexcusable and could only arise from the breakdown of culture and the crude reactions of men of violent nature. War was the ultimate degradation of man. "He who has slain numbers should mourn and wear sack-cloth." "The appeal to arms is the lowest form of virtue. Rewards and punishments are the lowest form of education. Ceremonies and laws are the lowest form of government."[15]

Non-violence, however, is not based on weakness or cowardice, but is only possible in those possessing the true courage of restraint and the intelligence to overcome the elementary and immature tendency to retaliation. It has sustained power as opposed to the disintegrating and dissipating qualities of violence. The incidence of violence in any of its forms is also symptomatic of a breakdown in either society or the individual, be it international murder by states, as in war, or in personal violence. No society in which such uncontrolled acts occur can be regarded as civilized, for civilization implies respect for others, either personally, or in their property or opinions, and demands certain standards of self-control and forbearance which, in turn, produce peace and contentment in the body politic. The old Chinese habit of "face saving" had much sound sense behind it. Where both parties acknowledged the fault and accepted the blame, no rancour was left behind to ferment resentment and future violence.

Violence is essentially unbalanced, it is an over-emphasis and, as such, must inevitably accentuate the qualities which give rise to more violence. Aggression can only breed aggression and provoke a violent and often dangerous response. The same applies to violence of emotions or convictions which leads to persecution and so strengthens opposition. Religious sects which have tried to place the whole, and unbalanced, emphasis on one aspect instead of accepting life in its entirety have produced their opposites. What should be love has turned to hate and strife. As has been said, Taoism advocates requiting good for evil, a doctrine which did not find favor with Confucius who argued that if one repaid evil with good, with what did one repay kindness? He maintained that one should "reward enmity with justice and kindness", whereas Lao Tzu said that the true man rose above the distinctions of either.

Once identified with, united to, the rest of creation, violence becomes both absurd and impossible, for it is then realized that to harm or hurt anyone else is to inflict that injury on oneself, and who but a psychopath would do that? So, too, any violence against or violation of nature ultimately rebounds on the exploiter or "conqueror" of nature.

[13] *Chuang Tzu* XVII, trans. Giles.
[14] *Tao Te Ching* XXIII, trans. Waley.
[15] *Chuang Tzu* XIII, trans. Giles.

7. THE NATURAL

The Sage is, above all, the wholly natural man. "Those who do not shrink from the natural, nor wallow in the artificial; they are near to perfection."[1] The artificial is the preoccupation with the things of the manifest world, and to be concerned with it is termed "going beyond the mark", as do people who "toil, putting together more wealth than they can use" and "officials who turn night into day in their endeavors to compass their ends".[2] "It has been said that the natural abides within, the artificial without. Virtue abides in the natural."[3]

The emphasis on the natural in Taoism must not be mistaken for any "back to nature" movement. One cannot go back to what one already is. It is, rather, "to find one's true nature", to get rid of the layers of the artificial and bring to light that which has always been there. Nor is it any form of naturalism, for Nature herself is never worshiped. The Nature which man can observe is only the kaleidoscopic outward manifestation of the great inner power behind manifestation. It is this power which is the Nature of the Taoist. It is the paradisial state in which man's nature is good and in true balance and therefore in harmony with all life; his faculties are then in perfect order, fulfilling all potentialities. In asserting man's "original goodness" Taoism maintains that he is capable, here and now, of a return to this paradisial state of perfection. Paradise is not permanently lost, it is an internal state which, at the moment of enlightenment, can be brought to actuality. It is to realize, to the fullest extent, the sum of all spiritual and metaphysical as well as human possibilities.

Man is not an alien in the world, he is a traveler, but one who is fully conscious of the conditions around him, who is, or should be, part of them and vitally interested, yet views all *sub specie aeternitatis*.[4] The natural implies a fearless contemplation of infinity while moving in the finite. "We must obey the laws of earth if we wish to know the truths of the spirit."[5] "Everything has its own nature. It can be developed according to its nature, but not shaped or forced against it."[6] It is to know the perfect fitness of things. "If a man sleeps in a damp place, he will have a pain in his loins and half his body will be as if it were dead; but will it be so with an eel? If he is at the top of a tree he will be frightened and all of a tremble; but will it be so with a monkey? Among these three, who knows the right way of habitation?"[7] "Play music in wild places and birds and beasts and fishes will take themselves off—only men will gather to hear it".[8]

In the natural there is a total co-operation with life. Modern man tends to be an observer rather than a partaker, he imagines

[1] *Chuang Tzu* XIX, trans. Giles.

[2] Ibid., XVIII.

[3] Ibid., XVII.

[4] Editor's Note: "under the aspect of eternity".

[5] Radhakrishnan, *India and China*.

[6] Wang Pi, *Commentaries*.

[7] *Chuang Tzu* II, trans. Fung Yu-lan.

[8] *Chuang Tzu* XVIII, trans. Giles.

Chang Feng (active 1636-1662), *Looking Towards the Waterfall*, Ming dynasty he can stand apart from life, view it from the outside, look at it with an analytical mind, or, worse still, with the roving eye of curiosity. It is impossible to be in accord with a world one regards as wholly other, it is to be a split personality, the modern schizophrenia. The merely analytical approach is the masculine, *yang*, by itself an arid intellectual function, while that of pure feeling is the *yin* "humid" reaction. Both must be kept in balance and supplement each other. Head and heart, reason and feeling, dry and humid, are all equally useless and destructive of harmony unless held in equilibrium. The observation of nature, however acute and detailed, is not the same as entering into understanding through intuition and being. "The Sage … does not view things as apprehended by himself, subjectively, but transfers himself into the position of the thing viewed. This is called using the Light."[9] To observe analytically is to set a thing apart, to make it other than oneself and to admit an element of patronage. It is as man enters into the nature of things and when he begins to appreciate the thing in itself, not as a tool or something useful to him personally, that he first transcends the animal. Conversely, he descends below the animal when he sets out to exploit nature. Once he has become divorced from nature and has lost the sense of communion with all things, the Oneness, he starts on the downward path which leads to destruction, not only of nature but of his own spiritual life, for the two are intimately associated; as he kills nature, so he kills himself. If he ill-treats and enslaves her he inflicts injury on and enslaves himself. The natural man is one who "is always in accordance with Nature, and does nothing to increase artificially that which is already in his life." Nor does he "inflict internal injury upon himself with desires and aversions".[10]

The Sage lived in close touch and co-operation with nature and though often a solitary or hermit was not necessarily so. Often, like the Hindu "forest dwellers", he had served the state, or humanity, in some capacity before retiring to the wild places to live a life of contemplation. His attitude was not world-renouncing, but looking at life and rejecting the artificial and sophisticated in favor of that which is real and of primary importance. It is a question of values. The contempt for money and pity for the rich arises from so simple an exercise as watching the effects of riches: the strained and anxious striving, the total inability to be idle, to relax and enjoy living, the fear of loss, the barriers interposed and suspicions engendered, the endless, futile, and ever-accelerated search for more and more hectic pleasure and time killing. The only way to "kill" time is to get beyond and out of it. One might quote Lin Yu-tang on the American vices, but for "American" read most of the Western world. "The three great American vices seem to be efficiency, punctuality, and the desire for achievement and success. They are the things that make the Americans so unhappy and so nervous. They steal from them their inalienable right to loafing and cheat them of many a good, idle, and beautiful afternoon.… The tempo of modern industrial life forbids this kind of glorious and magnificent idling. But worse than that, it imposes upon us a different conception of time as measured by the clock, and eventually turns the human being into a clock himself."[11]

[9] *Chuang Tzu* II, trans. Fung Yu-lan.

[10] Ibid., V.

[11] Lin Yu-tang, *The Importance of Living* (published by William Heinemann).

Ch'en Ju Yen (c. 1331-1371), *Mountains of the Immortals*, Yüan dynasty, late 14th century

As Meister Eckhart says, there is no intrinsic harm in the possession and enjoyment of riches provided one is equally capable of accepting life without them, and in this he exposes the rot at the core of riches, for the ordinary man, once he has acquired them, worships at the shrine of Mammon henceforth and while he is engaged in worship of this god life slips by unseen, unappreciated, unlived. The Sage extracts the maximum experience from his passing through this world since he is fully involved with the universal as well as the particular. "In self-esteem without self-conceit, in moral culture without chastity … in government without rank or fame, in retirement without solitude, in health without hygiene—there we have oblivion absolute coupled with possession of all things, an infinite calm which becomes an object to be attained by all."[12]

Withdrawal from the world was no asceticism. Even if a hermit, the true Sage soon gathered disciples round himself if he were known to have the Tao. The Sages, artists, and poets who retired to the wilds seemed to have a genius for friendship, sharing their wisdom, music, and poetry and delighting in company just as often as enjoying solitude, and so, in their lives, maintaining the *yin-yang* harmony of inward and outward movement. The ex-

[12] *Chuang Tzu* XV, trans. Giles.

Conversation in a Cave, anonymous, Southern Sung dynasty, c. 1220-1250

changes and discussions between sages and artists were not exercises in the subtleties of the dialectician. Chuang Tzu regarded knowledge for knowledge's sake as a source of endless trouble. Worldly knowledge is "artificial intelligence" and facts about facts, involving nothing beyond the rational mind and the world of phenomena. "Do not develop your artificial intelligence, but develop that which is from Heaven."[13] External knowledge leads

[13] Ibid., XIX.

to multiplicity, dissipation, and confusion. "Knowledge of the Great Unity—this alone is perfection."[14] In knowledge we get "more and more", in Tao we "get less and less". Erudition consists of acquiring and retaining a mass of information which is static and concerned with the past and historicity. "The past is dead while the present is living. If one attempts to handle the living with the dead, one certainly will fail."[15] Wisdom demands a fluid attitude of life-understanding and is dynamic and, being concerned with life in its entirety, it cannot be divorced from the spiritual. Frithjof Schuon writes, "People no longer sense the fact that the quantitative richness of a knowledge—of any kind of knowledge—necessarily entails an interior impoverishment unless accompanied by a spiritual science able to maintain balance and re-establish unity."[16] Knowledge for knowledge's sake produces the dry-as-dust pedagogue who not only lacks understanding but is vastly pleased with his limited condition. Chuang Tzu laughs at him. "You make a show of your knowledge in order to startle fools. You cultivate yourself in contrast to the degradation of others and you blaze along as though the sun and moon were under your arms, consequently you cannot avoid trouble."[17] And again—"You cannot speak of the ocean to a well frog; the creature of a narrow sphere. You cannot speak of ice to a summer insect; the creature of a season. You cannot speak of Tao to a pedagogue; his scope is too restricted."[18]

The Sage does not teach by imparting knowledge but by example. "The true Sage keeps his knowledge within him, while men in general set forth theirs in argument, in order to convince each other.... Perfect Tao does not declare itself, nor does perfect argument express itself in words".[19] The Sage has the power of "speaking without words", which is the penetrating influence unconsciously but inevitably exerted by the enlightened man. He has no need to "exert" influence, he naturally draws people to himself. "The people follow him who has the Tao as the hungry follow food they see before them."[20] Also, "Men cling to him as children who have lost their mother; they rally round him as wayfarers who have missed the road."[21] Because he fulfills all the potentialities of man, he has perfect understanding. "He who is naturally in sympathy with men, to him all men come", and "Those whose hearts are in a state of repose give forth divine radiance."[22] "All things to him are as One. Yet he knows not that this is so. It is simply nature. In the midst of action he remains the same. He makes Heaven his guide, and men make him theirs."[23] Confucius says, also, "The Sage is not unhappy if men do not know him. He is unhappy if he does not know men."

The deprecation of merely academic knowledge and past history is not a break with all knowledge and tradition. There is a constant reference to "the Sages of old" in both Taoism and Confucianism and to learning from them, for this is the inner knowledge of the Tao, which is traditional and living from age to age, in contradistinction to the flash-in-the-pan "philosophies" which follow

[14] Ibid., XXIV.

[15] Kuo Hsiang, *Commentaries on Chuang Tzu.*

[16] Schuon, *Treasures of Buddhism.*

[17] *Chuang Tzu* XX, trans. Giles.

[18] Ibid., XVII.

[19] *Chuang Tzu* II, trans. Fung Yu-lan.

[20] *Kwan Tzu*, seventh century B.C.

[21] *Chuang Tzu*, XII, trans. Giles.

[22] Ibid., XXIII.

[23] Ibid., XXV.

each other in quick succession, become fashionable, then outmoded, and are anything but perennial. These boost the ego in trying to find some "original" form of thinking, and here again we see the current trend in the misuse of words. "Original" is, properly, that which is attached to its origins, not that which arises from some individual psyche, or something floating about at the mercy of every wind that blows. The traditional[24] attaches man to his origins and should provide him with stability, but not immobility, and show him the way to realization in following the Sage who, having harmonized and transcended all opposites in himself, is capable of living in harmony in the world, getting full value from, and finding full significance in, life and imparting his teaching by example so that others, too, may find that though "we are born first into the world of nature and necessity, we are to be reborn into a world of spirit and freedom.... We are not only social beings but pilgrims in eternity."[25]

The same power of example in the Sage should also be evident in the ruler of the country, he should be the living example of living in accordance with the rules of nature, so that ruler, ruled, and nature are one. The evils of misrule lie with the rulers, not the ruled. Confucius said that "In archery there is a resemblance to the man of true breeding. If he misses the target he looks for the cause in himself." So it should be with those in authority. As is the case with morality, so with the enforcement of a multiplicity of laws, comes the breakdown of the natural state of simplicity and spontaneity and the rule of right becomes lost in the rule of might. Interference by the state, prohibitions and legislation ultimately encourage and increase the evils they were designed to prevent. Lawmaking should be kept to a minimum as it destroys the freedom of the people and the individual and reduces them to slave status. Once so reduced they cease to be capable of thinking for themselves and are easily led by any subversive influences, they become wholly dependent on rules and regulations and mistake the means for the end. In Taoist phraseology, they lose the way. "The rulers of old set off all success to the credit of their people, attributing all failure to themselves.... If any matter fell short of achievement, they turned and blamed themselves." In what follows, Chuang Tzu is as up-to-date as the current year—"Not so the rulers of today. They conceal a thing and blame those who cannot see it.... They inflict heavy burdens and chastise those who cannot bear them ... and the people, feeling that their powers are inadequate, have recourse to fraud. For when there is much fraud about how can the people be otherwise than fraudulent?... If their knowledge is insufficient, they will have recourse to deceit. If their means are insufficient, they will steal. And for such robbery and theft, who is really responsible?"[26] To which, today, the answer is—any government in power anywhere.

The ruler is adjured to govern "as one would cook a small fish", that is, with a light touch and not overdoing it! This attitude of non-interference is in no way the equivalent of anarchy since it is based on the qualities of the Sage-ruler and, while it tilts at such

[24] "By a Tradition is meant not merely a historical continuity, and still less a blind observance of customs bereft of their former meaning, but a transmission of principles of more-than-human origin, effectively applied in every field of thought and action." (Aristide Messinesi, in *Art and Thought*)

[25] Radhakrishnan, *India and China*.

[26] *Chuang Tzu* XXV, trans. Giles.

Opposite: Wen Cheng-ming (1470-1559), *Noble Scholars in a Solitary Ravine*, Ming dynasty

Tai Chin, *Seeking the Tao in a Cavern-Heaven*, Ming dynasty, 15th century

things as social conventions, moralities, and over-government by the state, it is not a *carte blanche* for licence, but to live in a natural and unsophisticated way. There is the story of old Camelback, who was a highly successful gardener. People wanted to know the secret of his success, but he denied having any particular method other than fostering natural tendencies. "In planting trees be careful to set the roots straight, to smooth the earth around, to use good mold and to ram it down well. Then don't touch them, don't think about them, don't go and look at them, but leave them alone to take care of themselves and nature will do the rest. I only avoid trying to make trees grow.... Others are for ever running backwards and forwards to see how they are growing, sometimes scratching them to make sure they are still alive, or shaking them to see if they are sufficiently firm in the ground, thus constantly interfering with the natural bias of the tree and turning their affection and care into an absolute bane and curse. I only don't do these things. That's all." Asked if his principles could be applied to government, he replied: "Ah, I only understand gardening, government isn't my trade. Still, in the village where I live, the officials are for ever issuing all kinds of orders, as if greatly compassionating the people, though really to their utter injury. Morning and night the underlings come round and say: 'His Honor bids us urge on your ploughing, hasten your planting, and superintend your harvest. Do not delay with your spinning and weaving. Take care of your children. Rear poultry and pigs. Come together when the drum beats.' Thus are the poor people badgered from morning till night. We have not a moment to ourselves. How could anyone flourish and develop naturally under such circumstances?"

Taoism in no way rejects the world of the senses and ordinary life but keeps them in perspective, using them as a means to transcend themselves. Ignoring the sense-world would be to kill the very arts to which Taoism gave birth with such eminent success. The senses are, as is said in *The Doctrine of the Mean*, the instruments of a vital moving power in man which it is his duty to develop. The world of the senses is neither sought nor denied, but accepted. "Affection and aversion for the objects of sense abide in the senses, but let none come under the dominion of those two; they are his adversaries."[27] Sense data and empirical methods are certainly necessary for gaining knowledge and perspective in the phenomenal world, but they are by nature naive and limited and cannot deal with the non-physical knowledge and powers manifested in the mind and spirit; everything earthly must by definition fall short of the ideal; all sense perception is relative and imperfection is inherent in manifestation and multiplicity. True, a vast amount of data can be amassed via the senses, but this is a matter of quality and quantity is irrelevant. It is the greatest of illusions to imagine that man is no more than his body and senses; in sense perception one sees only results and consequences, not the thing-in-itself. Plato taught that man's elements are in disorder but are capable of being harmonized on the principle of a scale, the senses being the lowest and the World of Ideas the highest.

The senses relay only a limited amount and type of facts, drawn, it is reasonable to suppose, from a larger and unlimited source. The experiences they transmit tend to a pre-establishment and pre-judging of ideas about any person, thing, or situation and to fitting everything into an accepted or acceptable framework, producing a mental outlook which is more interested in the shape, color and position of each piece of a jigsaw rather than the total picture built. It is not possible to get an overall picture through the senses alone any more than it is possible to see and understand the whole of a river by scooping up and analyzing a basin of water taken from it. Mencius says man loses his human qualities and becomes an animal when he lives in the sense world alone. This, however, is not altogether fair to the animal, since a noble animal often exhibits finer qualities than an ignoble man; also, his senses are in many ways superior to man's and he has the advantage of having kept the powers of intuition which in man have largely atrophied. Chinese philosophy maintained that the senses should be a small part (*hsiao c'i*) of man. They not only convey knowledge in a limited way but in everyday life are responsible for endless distraction and a dissipation of energy and mind. Hinduism and Buddhism regard them as totally unreliable while the Eleatic School of Greece condemned them outright as a court of appeal but admitted that they have a limited but important part to play; it is only in regarding them as absolute that the fatal mistake is made. "If you want to follow the doctrine of the One do not rage against the world of senses. Only by accepting the world of senses can you share in True Perception."[28]

[27] *Bhagavad Gita*, III.34

[28] Takakusu XLVIII. 376.

Wu Wei, *The Perfect Man of the Northern Sea*, Ming dynasty, 15th century

8. THE GREAT TRIAD

The Taoist Great Triad of Heaven-Man-Earth is not to be taken in the naturalist sense of Sky-Earth divinities. Heaven represents the Spirit or Essence, Earth the Substance, and Man the synthesis of both and mediator between them, himself partaking of the dual nature of Heaven and Earth. "Man", here, is not "the man in the street", but the Taoist Sage or Confucian Perfect Man, who was symbolized by the Emperor, the Son of Heaven. The Perfect Man is the achievement of the potential of human nature in all its *yin-yang* possibilities. As synthesis and mediator he occupies the central position and demonstrates the underlying unity of apparent opposites, leading back to the center from the dispersion and fragmentation of the manifest and formal world, resolving the *yin-yang* dualism in the Tao. In the phenomenal world, spirit and substance are held together by the third element, the body, in which the two unite. As the intermediary, man has the qualities of both Heaven and Earth in his nature, the urges and instincts of the animal and aspirations to the divine and can, when possessed of Tao, compensate and reconcile both. "Heaven, Earth, and Man are the basis of all creation. Heaven produces them, Earth nourishes them, and Man completes them."[1]

The Triad bears no direct relationship to the Trinities of the theistic religions, though, to a certain extent, it partakes of the Father-Mother-Son symbolism in that the last, here, is also the product of the interaction of the first two, and Heaven and Earth are said to be "the Father and Mother of all things"; but this is not a personal trinity.

Chinese ideogram of the Great Triad

Man, as central, is involved in all the symbolism of the center. He is the meeting place for, and gives access to, both the celestial and the chthonic worlds and is seen as the balance and harmony of the play between Heaven and Earth. As with the *yin-yang* symbolism, here, too, is met the significance and auspiciousness of odd numbers. Three, the first odd number, and also indivisible, emphasizes both man's position in the cosmos and his obligation to maintain equilibrium, thus the Perfect Man must not be onesided or "eccentric", but must have an equal and harmonious blending of both Heaven and Earth in his nature. His position is also symbolized in the trigrams, of which, as has been seen, the upper line represents Heaven, the lower Earth, with Man in the middle. Here also, we have the symbolism of the sacred tortoise, one of the four "spiritually endowed" animals, as its carapace is taken as the dome of heaven, its lower shell the

[1] *The Chung Yung*, from *The Book of Rites*.

earth, while its body in the center is man with his ability to expand outwardly and contract inwardly in the dualistic world.

Taoism and Confucianism were the inheritors and custodians of an ancient and primordial tradition, handed down from the Golden Age or paradisial state. Hierarchical in form, it was graded to meet the needs of all strata of society, so that the simplest were no more excluded from participation than the most intellectual. At the head of this society was the emperor, symbolizing the Perfect Man and the meeting point of Heaven and Earth, Son of Heaven and Regent on Earth (the only emperor never to wear a sword). When giving audience, the emperor's throne faced south; Chinese cosmology and astronomy being based on the polar stars, the emperor thus assumed the central position in the kingdom on earth, reflecting the position of the Pole Star in the heavens. The reason that China called herself the Middle Kingdom was that she represented the terrestrial reflection of the celestial Middle Kingdom. In the person of the emperor, and ruler, should be demonstrated the impartiality and justice of Heaven and of Nature, violation of the laws of either bringing automatic retribution. The ruler must be "impartial and equitable". "The Perfect Man is like Heaven, which covers everything without partiality. The partial man brings confusion and anarchy into the world under heaven."[2] This impartiality is not only a quality necessary in the emperor, or any ruler, but also in individual man as ruler of himself, which is, indeed, the most difficult of all in that it necessitates the control of the selfish demands of the ego. Only as he conforms to the laws of Heaven and Nature can man take his true central place and become the Sage, able to assume his place as mediator. It is when he fails to perform his function as mediator and arrogates to himself the role of a god, or devil, that trouble starts, for example, as when he attempts to use nature for his own ends, or when he aims not at the selfless state of the Sage, but at the super-ego of the superman. Undeterred by the example of Nietzsche's breakdown in madness and the political monstrosity which arose from his cult of the superman, there are still worshipers at the humanistic shrine of the would-be super mental-physical creature, the unbalanced man of Earth, trying to exclude Heaven.

Symbolically, the union of Heaven and Earth in the *yin* and *yang* is also the squaring of the circle, and the earliest references to moral codes (which were pre Taoist-Confucianist) in China are symbolized in terms of the square and the compass and the level. Man, as the result of the union of Heaven and Earth, the circle and the square, should exhibit the perfection of both. "The balance revolving gave birth to the circle; what the circle involves is a square."[3] The poet Li Sao calls the crooked the standard of "showy elegance", a mark of a decadent society divorced from the natural, while "squareness" was integrity. But according to Chuang Tzu, all distinctions between curved and straight, the crooked and the square, should be resolved in unity.

As René Guénon so frequently insists, the Cartesian dualism of body-mind bears little resemblance to reality and has had an unfortunate influence on the whole of Western thought. The ternary division of body, soul, and spirit, on the other hand, is not only the most general, but at the same time the most

[2] *Kwan Tzu*, Book XIII.

[3] From the *Ch'ien-han-lu-li-chih*.

Opposite: The Purple Tenuity Emperor of the North Pole Star and Attendants, Ming dynasty, c. 1460, Pao Ning Temple, Shan Hsi province

北極紫微大帝眾
左第二十一

The Chinese character for Shou ("long life"), composed to resemble the Taoist "internal circulation" diagram

simple that can be found in defining the constitution of a living being, and one which is present in all great traditions. Man is himself a microcosm, composed of the dualistic nature of the *yin-yang* and, reconciling and unifying these in himself, is the masculine spirit and feminine soul united, from which the third, the son, the unifying principle, emerges. As the reconciling and cognizing factor, man is also the mean; he stands not only between Heaven and Earth, but also between time and eternity. He is the prisoner of time until he, literally, sees through it and becomes the denizen of eternity when he sees face-to-face. As the mean he must keep all balance in the world, and it is his greatest crime, today, bringing with it inevitable retribution, that man who should keep the balance in nature is the greatest disturber of that balance. If he falls short of the Tao and the *Te*, he loses his power, becomes a non-entity, and does not play his proper part in the world, his actions and non-actions are equally ineffective. On the other hand, if he goes beyond the mean and regards himself as Lord of Creation, as is arrogantly assumed by humanism, he again loses the mid-point, the Center, and becomes eccentric and unbalanced. Nor can he turn his back on mankind and abdicate from life without failing in his position as mediator. Such a man, Chuang Tzu says, "has drowned himself on dry land".[4] "It is only the man who is entirely real in this world who has the capacity to give full development to his human nature. If he has that capacity it follows that he has the capacity to give full development to the natures of all species of things. Thus it is possible for him to be assisting the transforming and nourishing work of Heaven-and-Earth. That being so, it is possible for him to be part of a trinity of Heaven, Earth, and himself."[5] "The *yang* represents Heaven's forbearingness, the *yin* Heaven's exigency, the Mean, Heaven's utility."[6]

In alchemy the triad also represents sulfur, quicksilver, and salt. These terms, again, must not be interpreted materially but as spiritual principles. Sulfur as *yang*, solar, fire, symbolizes the Will of Heaven, the active principle. Quicksilver as *yin*, lunar, the waters, is the passive and limiting power. Salt, the "crystallization", as the result of the action and reaction of the *yin-yang*, is the neutral zone in which the contrary forces are stabilized and reconciled. This also represents the work within the individual.

[4] *Chuang Tzu* XXV, trans. Giles.
[5] *The Chung Yung*, trans. Fung Yu-lan.
[6] Tung Chung-shu.

In alchemy the pairs of opposites are at first antagonistic and later unified through the "work", but in Taoist alchemy the antagonism is not stressed so much as the interaction and co-operation of the two principles, male and female, sun and moon, spiritual and temporal powers, red and white, sulfur and quicksilver. Nor did Chinese alchemy employ the symbolism of gold to the same extent as other branches of the work. Gold with its associations with money and commerce, was considered vulgar and beneath the notice of the scholar and outside the range of interest of the Sage; the Chinese alchemist originally belonged to the scholarly and cultured class. It was longevity and the elixir of immortality that chiefly engaged their attention. Alchemy is essentially initiatory and so its ideas are in line with the normal practice of Taoism, which presupposes the transmission of esoteric knowledge from master to pupil and a discipline of meditation and contemplation. A sharp distinction must be drawn between the mystical alchemy of the scholar, working on an entirely spiritual plane, and the debased alchemy which appeared later in the hands of an ignorant priesthood whose "alchemy" was largely indistinguishable from magic, spiritualism, and shamanistic practices. The ignorant and foolish misunderstood the "work" of alchemy and looked for the making of material, instead of spiritual, riches or "wealth". They were called "charcoal burners" by the genuine alchemists of the West, and "blowers" in the East. They labored under the delusion that the work was material, that lead could be turned into solid gold instead of into the pure gold of the effulgence of spiritual enlightenment. The transmutation sought was, in fact, that of man himself from his "base" metal or leaden state into the perfection of the light symbolized by gold, a purely inner work of transformation. The immortality, the "changing skins" sought in the elixir was enlightenment, realization of the Tao, changing from one state to another, passing from death to life, "from the unreal to the real", that "out of darkness one may go forth into light". The old, ignorant nature must be dissolved and transmuted into the

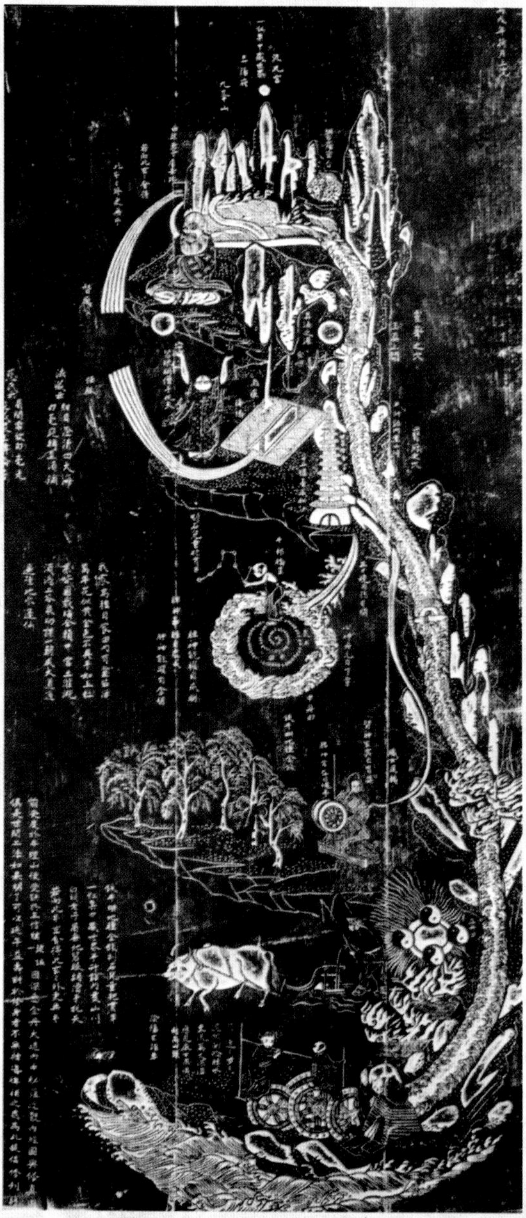

Diagram of the subtle body, mapping the inner alchemy, Ch'ing dynasty, c. 1886

Shou Lao, star god of longevity, late Ming dynasty, c. 1589

new man; this is the "chaotic" state in alchemy in which dissolution takes place within the sealed vessel, often symbolically egg-shaped, and is employed in Taoism to represent the state of return to the undifferentiated attained in mysticism in the abolition of duality and the return to the Tao. Here it is of interest to note that, in China, the butterfly is the symbol *par excellence* of immortality, having, between the states of earthbound caterpillar and ethereal butterfly, gone through a process of complete dissolution before rebirth into the winged state of freedom.

There is a constant *yin-yang* reaction in the realm of duality, the never-ending interplay between the *solve et coagula*, in which the volatile must be stabilized and the coagulate dissolved. This is also, as Guénon says,[7] the alternation of "lives" and "deaths" in the sense that "life for the body is death for the spirit" and vice versa, bringing "life to death and death to life", or, "spiritualizing the body and embodying the spirit". "In leaving the state of non-manifestation to pass into manifestation (which is, properly speaking, the "cosmological" point of view), it is 'condensation or coagulation which naturally first occurs'." This also demonstrates why the *yin* must always precede the *yang* since the emergence from the non-manifest state of the Tao into duality necessitates the *yin* "condensation" of the *prima materia*. The androgyne is the *yin-yang* regaining complete and absolute unity in the Tao; it is not an annihilation or extinction, but the immortality of the perfection of the One.

The Taoist-Buddhist doctrine of "the active essence of non-action and the passive essence of action" runs through all alchemical traditions as the spiritual work of transmuting and ennobling the soul, the soul being the "substance" worked upon, the spirit expressing itself in form. This involves both the existential and the essential. "When there is conglomeration, form comes into being; when there is dispersion, it comes to an end. This is what we mortals mean by beginning and end. But although, for us, in a state of conglomera-

[7] *The Great Triad* (published by Quinta Essentia).

tion, this condensation into form constitutes a beginning, and its dispersion an end, from the standpoint of dispersion it is void and calm that constitute the beginning, and condensation into form the end. Hence there is perpetual alternation in what constitutes beginning and end, and the underlying Truth is that there is neither any beginning nor any end at all."[8] This was the pure metaphysical teaching of alchemy, but it was the "blowers" who were responsible for the later decadence of Taoist alchemy. Many accounts of the search for the Isles of the Blessed and the Pill of Immortality are entirely allegorical and hide the serious pursuit of spiritual knowledge, of mystical states and the attainment of the center, the perfection which cinnabar, the golden flower, the crystallization of light, the essence of immortality, symbolized; just as "riding on the winds" or "wandering in the clouds" is the metaphysical state of freedom of the spirit. As Lieh Tzu said when he had freed himself from all sensation, he "drifted from East to West at the will of the wind like the leaf of a tree, or a withered twig", until in the end he was "uncertain whether the wind was bearing me or it was I who carried the wind".

The spiritual quest for the immortality of oneness in the Tao degenerated into the material search for personal immortality in finding the elixir or pill which would confer this condition on man. It appears that many of the experimenters were actually poisoned and died in the process, though in some cases the results were more felicitous, as with Wei Poyang who made some pills, took some himself and gave some to his dog and a favorite disciple, with the immediate effect of all three being translated to the Realm of the Immortals!

Liu Hai crossing the sea carrying his toad and the gourd bottle of elixir, Ming dynasty

There was also the instance of Huai-nan Tzu who wrote a treatise on alchemy and was said to have discovered the pill of immortality: he took it and forthwith ascended to the heavens, an event which took place in daylight, in the presence of witnesses. In the euphoria of the moment he dropped the jar containing the rest of the pills, and his dog and his hens, picking them up, all took off to heaven after

[8] *The Book of Lieh Tzu*, trans. Giles.

Dreaming of Immortality, attributed to Chou Ch'en (active c. 1500-1535), Ming dynasty

him on the spot.

After the life of a founder and his immediate followers, the first purity of a doctrine suffers at the hands of those who have found the teaching too hard or too austere and who seek to turn it into an easier way. Mankind is naturally lazy and looks for something more easily understood or which can be manipulated to suit its tastes. Lao Tzu's teaching of the Tao was, as he said, inexpressible in any case, and the ideas of self-emptiness, the void, *wu-wei* and the emphasis laid on pure being were too metaphysical and intellectual a standard for the understanding and taste of the average man who prefers the familiar terrain of moral codes and creeds.

Decadence set in after the Sung dynasty when, under the Wei, those who professed Taoism developed a nihilistic attitude, abdicated from the world, drowned their disillusionment in wine, and formed a school of artists, philosophers, and poets known as "the Seven Sages of the Bamboo Grove". They were men of keen wit, but who lacked, in their egoistic world-renunciation, the balance of the true Sage. Taoism fell gradually from the sublime metaphysics of a noble and spiritual culture to the lowest form of popular superstitions and beliefs in all manner of gods and demons. From being non-theistic, it developed a vast pantheon of gods. It catered for the innate superstition found in human nature and so beloved by it, so that the pure teaching of union with the Tao fell into the crude cult of longevity and personal immortality.

The element of distortion and exaggeration must always be present in decadence, so from having no Heaven and Hell, both were established with all their most lurid concomitants. Instead of mastering his own nature, the

Taoist, now a priest and magician, set out to master the forces of nature. He claimed that he could, literally, ride on the backs of dragons and fly on cranes, symbolic of the messengers between gods and men. All these were physical interpretations of that which had once been the symbol of the liberated mind and powers of the spirit, just as the Taoist sword juggler of the theater and market-place was the degenerate form of the symbol of the knife-bridge or ladder of the perilous and difficult passage to enlightenment. The magician concentrated on levitation, walking on waters, immunity from burning by fire, and generally sank into shamanism, complete with mediumistic communication with the dead, witchcraft, demonology, and all the extravagances of extreme psychism. The body was cultivated, not to use it as an aid to the spirit, but in order to preserve it for the maximum number of physical years. Indeed, at the conquest of China by the Mongols under Genghis Khan, the Taoist priests found themselves in complete accord with the shamanistic beliefs and practices of the conquerors and attached themselves to the new dynasty in considerable numbers.

The *yin-yang* principle also became decadent, as must happen, according to its own teaching, as soon as the balance is disturbed. The emperor no longer effectively united the

Shang Hsi (active late 15th century), *Four Immortals Honoring the God of Longevity*, Ming dynasty

temporal and spiritual powers, the latter being delegated to degenerate priests. In the temporal power decadence sets in when the state attempts to govern alone and usurp the functions of the spiritual power. The state then dominates and dictates instead of serving the good of its members. The *yin-yang* once out of balance, the two Great Powers declined from cosmic forces into mere good and evil, which, in turn, suggested the existence of good and evil spirits who, in the minds of the masses, can grow and multiply into a teeming world of spirits suggesting every form of good and bad emotion, desire, or passion known to man. Fear, no trace of which was present in pure Taoism since it arises solely from man's own imagination, was now rampant in popular worship and propitiations.

The only thing that could be said in favor of decadent Taoism was that it was still associated with some of its original humor and wit. The story is told of a scoundrel who, having a deep grudge against a wealthy man, sought out a famous magician and asked for his help. "I can send you demon soldiers and secretly cut him off", said the magician. "Yes, but his sons and grandsons would inherit", replied the other; "that won't do." "I can draw fire from heaven", said the magician, "and burn his house and valuables." "Even then", answered the man, "his landed property would remain; so that won't do." "Oh", cried the magician, "if your hate is so deep as all that I have something precious here which, if you can persuade him to avail himself of it, will bring him and his to utter ruin." He thereupon gave his delighted client a tightly closed package, which, on being opened, was seen to contain a pen. "What spiritual power is in this?" asked the man. "Ah", sighed the magician, "you evidently do not know how many have been brought to ruin by the use of this little thing."[9]

In decadence the *yin* became demons of darkness and humidity and were in combat with the *yang* forces of fire and light, hence the symbolic use of fireworks, reputedly invented by the Chinese, used at all great spirit festivals to scare away the darkness and encourage the light, and the auspiciousness of all bright colors, red, representing fire, being the brightest and the luckiest. These propitiatory practices in turn degenerated even further into mere displays and the conventional usage of colors. All gods and spirits were also either *yin* or *yang*. The *kwei-shan* now became good and bad spirits instead of the originally pure guiding spirits. Deities of mountains and rivers, gods of agriculture, earth, and sky, and all local gods and even the spirits of ancestors became *yin* and *yang*, *kwei* or *shan*. Idolatry took over completely, though degenerate Taoist-Buddhist idolatry was no different from idolatry all the world over, for, as Schuon says, "Idolatry consists essentially in a reduction of the content of a symbol to the image itself in isolation from any metaphysical background."[10]

Lao Tzu's sublime teaching of the freedom of the spirit of the Sage degenerated into the physical and psychical licence of the fool. *Corruptio optimi pessima*.[11]

[9] Giles, *History of Chinese Literature* (published by D. Appleton-Century Co.).

[10] Schuon, *Treasures of Buddhism*.

[11] Editor's Note: "the corruption of the best is the worst of all."

Opposite: *Taoist Official of Water*, traditionally attributed to Wu Tao-tzu, Southern Sung dynasty, early 12th century

靜聽松風

9. ART

Possibly the first introduction the West had to Taoist principles was through art. The great flowering of Chinese art in the T'ang dynasty (the T'ang emperors claimed descent from Lao Tzu) and the following Sung dynasty, was mainly of Taoist inspiration and influence, Taoism being the court religion of that time. Certainly one of the most fundamental differences between East and West lies in the principles governing art. Far Eastern art has never been imitative, its interests lie in the metaphysical and spiritual rather than in the human realm. "It expresses a conception of the universe, a vision of wholeness, a liberation from the struggle for existence which subordinates everything to human interests and prejudices, a going-out of the spirit into solitudes, unafraid and exulting".[1] All traditional Chinese art is based on "the philosophy of repose". The artist usually abandoned public life and "in the way of enlightenment finds endless contentment".[2] There are pictures and poems of mountain-dwelling artists, gathering faggots in deep ravines by mountain streams, or collecting herbs on the hills, or fishing tranquily on rivers and lakes, living in the extreme simplicity of a thatched hut, in solitude, with no other sounds than the wind in the pines or the tumbling of the waters. Indeed, most Taoist poetry is like the soughing of the wind in the pines or the rustle of a breeze through a bamboo grove, so delicate a sound that one wonders if the whole were a dream, but mind and feeling have been stirred and it is left to experience to add to experience. Taoist art is mysticism made visible. Its transparent quality acts as a window on to worlds hidden from ordinary sight. It is the genius of suggestion rather than any exactly defined outward expression, suggestion which opens the door to infinity.

When one speaks of "art" in connection with the Far East it does not necessarily imply painting. The Chinese artist was not expected to be a man of one book, he was expected to be able to express his ideas in all three mediums of painting, poetry, and music and to translate them from one to the other. In any case Chinese poetry and music join, as a poem is sung rather than said. Every word is sonorous and no one could be a poet who had no ear for music, and "the Sages of old used to say that a poem is a picture without visible forms and that a painting is a poem which has put on form". Nor has art ever been a profession in China: it was a life. It was regarded as prostitution to sell works of art. Unless an artist could live his art, that is to be in accord with the rhythms and harmonies of life, he was regarded as of no more use than "a blocked flute through which no breath could pass". His art, like life, had to be a moving, flowing thing, it was no static perfection of form but a response. This is why Chinese painting and poetry suggest, imply, and interpret the moods and lessons of nature rather than record events or capture past scenes. Nothing is

[1] L. Binyon, *Chinese Art* (published by B.T. Batsford).
[2] Tsen Ts'an.

Opposite: Ma Lin (c. 1180-1256), *Listening to the Wind in the Pines*, Southern Sung dynasty, 1246

ever baldly stated or portrayed, but conveyed by suggestion, inference, metaphor, or simply empty space. In using the power of suggestion the artist, as with the teaching of the Sages, draws the onlooker in and makes him one with the rhythms of nature and the inner world.

The flowing, rhythmic quality of Taoist art also inferred the ever-changing and transitory nature of the world, the impermanence of any moods or circumstances. The empty space, so effectively employed, symbolizes the inner experience, and its use, according to Chinese artists, requires more thought and care than the actual strokes of the brush, so that meditation becomes an essential part of all painting, of all art. This "emptiness" is also open-mindedness. "When a man is empty and without bias everything will contribute its wisdom to him."[3] Emptiness is a pre-requisite for receptivity and, on the mundane plane, for being of any value in receiving or perceiving. It is the emptiness of a cup, bowl, or vase which makes it of use; it is the space of doors and windows which lets in the light and gives access to other worlds. Though supported by a frame, the actual advantage and usefulness lies in the emptiness. Symbolically, man is the framework which, if full of himself, has no room for anything else and blocks the light and prevents movement and leaves no room for the Tao.

Clay is molded into vessels,
And because of the space where nothing exists we are able to use them as vessels.
Doors and windows are cut out of the walls of a house,
And because they are empty spaces we are able to use them.
Therefore, on the one hand we have the benefit of existence, and on the other we make use of non-existence.[4]

Emptiness, the Void, is a transcending of dualism. It is not a nihilistic conception and, like the *yin-yang*, does not admit of an either/or, a full or empty. "Tao causes fullness and emptiness, but is not either."[5] It is a plenitude, the pleroma, the fullness of completion, the final goal of enlightenment, symbolized by the perfection of the empty circle; the Void from which all emanates and to which all returns. "The True man is empty and is everything. He is unconscious and is everywhere. He thus mysteriously unifies his own self with its other." "Identify yourself with the Infinite. Make excursion into the Void. Exercise fully what you have received from nature, but gain nothing besides. In one word, be empty".[6] Taoism and Buddhism both teach the same doctrine of the Void. "Emptiness does not fail to illuminate and illumination does not fail to empty" is a Buddhist saying, but could just as well have come from any Taoist writer. Emptiness goes beyond imagery and in the last resort it is necessary to pass beyond even the concept of unity, beyond all concepts, to the Void.

The first canon of art, laid down by the Taoist painter Hsieh-ho, is that it should manifest "The life-movement of the spirit through the rhythm of things", also translated by Waley as "the operation of the spirit producing life's motion", or it may be called simply "rhythmic vitality". The outward charm of

[3] Kuo Hsiang, *Commentaries.*

[4] *Tao Te Ching* XI, trans. Ch'u Ta-kao (published by George Allen & Unwin).

[5] *Chuang Tzu* XXII, trans. Giles.

[6] *Chuang Tzu* VII, trans. Fung Yu-lan.

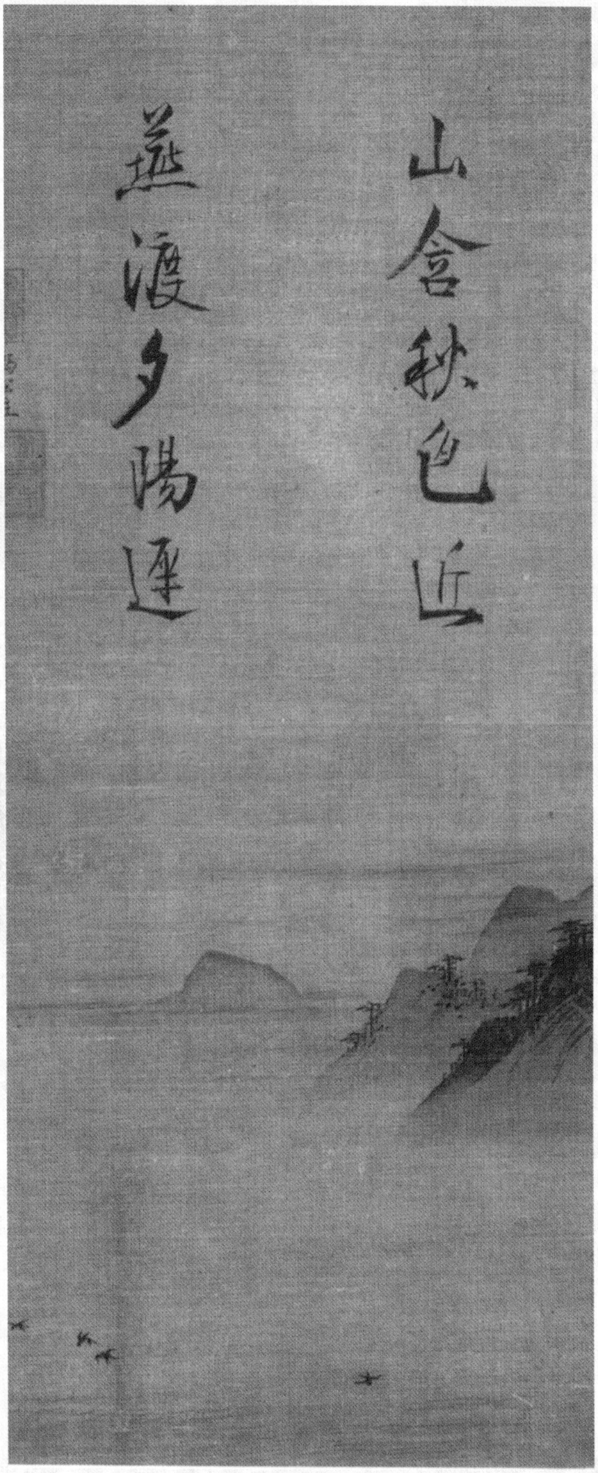

Ma Lin, *Sunset Landscape*, illustrating a couplet by the T'ang poet Wang Wei, Southern Sung dynasty

Taoist art holds a profound inner meaning, it leads beyond appearances and frees the spirit from the limitations of the senses, so that man is not confined to the solid, mundane view, but is placed in an elevated position from which he can see over valleys and hilltops to the distances beyond, which makes possible a subtle penetration of nature. "There is no art more lofty, more beneficent, more spiritual. There is none which helps to penetrate farther into the essence of things. It reveals to us the profound life behind appearances: each of its works, as it were, an apparition from a world more real than our world, an emanation from the Spirit which animates all things and rolls through all."[7]

Although largely concerned with scenes from nature, Chinese art was never a mere imitation of nature. Its aim was to reveal the deeper metaphysical content, pregnant with Tao. The artist did not go out to study nature, to use it as an escape, he did not go out to paint some imitation of a landscape and then return to his city studio at night; he lived with nature and was part and parcel of it. It was in no way external to himself, something to soothe and delight, but it was his very being, he was wholly identified with the cosmic rhythms and harmony in a total awareness. Taoist art was entirely metaphysical, art was a mirror of the soul. "The artist himself is the secret of his art." Taoism shared with Zoroastrianism the belief that all celestial things had earthly counterparts which are imbued with the spiritual power behind them, so that any art that lacks this spiritual quality and is designed merely to give pleasure is, as Plato says, only a toy. This is not to say that giving pleasure is no part of the function of art. Beauty is ever a

[7] Hovelaque, *China*.

Ma Lin, *Landscape with Great Pine*, Southern Sung dynasty, 13th century delight and there are entrancing accounts of artists' portrayals of nature which were so living that tigers were said to have walked out of pictures, birds taken flight, horses galloped away, and bamboo leaves and flowers moved at the breath of the beholder, not to mention the dragon which soared up into the sky as soon as the artist gave it eyes, and Wu Tao-tzu who wandered into his own painting, climbed a distant mountain and was never seen again!

Art awakens a response in the mind and soul and it is important that it should evoke the higher, not the lower, nature. Any artist must be responsible for the influence he exerts. If his work is designed to arouse evil qualities, he is just as responsible for the dissemination of evil as is the acknowledged criminal, indeed, more so, for he should know better. Taoist art evokes a spiritual and intellectual response and has in it no element of the emotional, passional, voluptuous, coarse, or violent. It never depicts purely physical power or the extremes of emotion in piety or sensuality, and the erotic and also the moralistic element is absent. There is an innate refinement and emotions are restrained, and if human figures appear they are in natural perspective, never dominating their surroundings and never passional. "If men's passions are deep, their divinity is shallow."[8] It is an ethereal art, pervaded with quiet contentment and repose and happiness in beauty. If any severity arises it is rather from an economy of line than from an austere philosophy of reserve; there is none of the forbidding gloom of some Western mountain scenes. It is always evocative of serenity and joyousness. By contrast, Western art appears solid, heavy, and congealed. Imbued with the universal and spiritual, Taoist art appeals to the universal and to the spirit. As A.K. Coomaraswamy says, "Secular art can only appeal to cliques.... This is, in fact, the diagnosis of our modern individualistic art, that seven-eighths of it is the work of men who ought to be servants and not masters; while the work of one-eighth (if there be so large a proportion of genius) is necessarily intelligible only to a very small audience."[9]

As the Sage had no use for the cult of personality, so the artist had no desire to develop his ego or impress by the personality. On the contrary, the aim of sacred art is to lose the self in the spirit. So the Taoist artist seldom "signed" paintings. His work was not the expression of some individual psyche, or as Albert Gleizes puts it, "personal physiological and psychological convulsions", but the working of the spirit in creativity: "production without possession, action without self-assertion, development without domination."[10] *The Dhammapada* says, "To wish that it may be made known that 'I was the author' is the thought of a man not yet adult." Also, "there cannot be an authorship of ideas, but only an entertainment, whether by one or many intellects is immaterial."[11]

"Art, as soon as it is no longer determined, illuminated, and guided by spirituality, lies at the mercy of the individual and purely psychical resources of the artist"; on the other hand, "the artist who lives in a traditional world ... works under the discipline or the inspiration of a genius which surpasses him".[12] It fol-

[8] *Chuang Tzu* VI, trans. Giles.

[9] Coomaraswamy, *Christian and Oriental Philosophy of Art* (published by Dover Publications, Inc.).

[10] Radhakrishnan, *India and China*.

[11] Coomaraswamy, *Christian and Oriental Philosophy of Art*.

[12] Schuon, "Concerning Forms of Art" in *Art and Thought*.

Wu Yüan-chih (fl. 1190-1196), *Red Cliffs*, Chin dynasty

lows that portraiture was little esteemed and largely ignored in traditional Chinese art. If people were represented it was usually sages in contemplation, whose images could act as an example of what man could, or should, be; of man enlightened and in repose and at one with the divine in nature and himself. Even then, the "portraits" were not lifelike, but represented the type rather than the person and often exaggerated certain features, such as the abnormally high head, symbolizing the mind-spirit aspect, or huge ears, indicating the ability to listen. There was no private portraiture, no "copy of a copy" to record the merely physical and egotistic. "Imitations only reproduce a dead form no longer animated by any living principle; they are only the thing produced, not the elusive spirit which produces."[13] Su T'ung-po said it was sufficient to portray the thoughts manifested; if the soul were not worth portraying there was no point in a portrait. It was symptomatic of the influence of an alien "culture", and the ultimate decay of Chinese art under the Manchus, that the Dowager Empress had her portrait painted by a Westerner and elaborately framed. The

[13] Hovelaque, *China*.

dying echoes of the former glory were seen in the Ming dynasty, where an ever-increasing imitativeness and effeteness crept in until it became wholly decadent with the Chins, when the traditional gave way to the merely technical, decorative, and charming. The beautiful was lost in the pretty and the deeply symbolic in the senseless, and the spirit was dead.

Not only was art never a profession and the artist never stooping to sell his work, but there was no commercial trade in art. Pictures and poems were given as a mark of close friendship or great respect. Only the decadent, or the commercially-minded and unscholarly merchant class, "collected" them. The anti-traditional attitude reaches its full shockingness when works of art attain a commercial value, being lumped together like so many pieces of merchandise, standing about for casual inspection like any prostitute or slave on the market, gaped at and bid for by people primarily concerned with the cash value or the enhancing of the collector's ego with the pride of possession, a situation utterly impossible in the ancient Chinese civilization.

Taoist art, concerned mainly with mountain scenery (landscape painting was called "mountain and water pictures", and mountains were regarded as composed of a more subtle substance than the earth of the plains), puts man into perspective, making him part of the natural scene. He is a small creature when compared with mountain vastness, so as a small figure he appears. He is not allowed to dominate the scene, nor is nature ever used merely as a background to show him off. Putting him into perspective is, however, a very different thing from dwarfing him; he is there in right proportion. A dwarf is an anomaly and out of balance and harmony, but so too is the man who is larger-than-life, using nature only to throw himself into relief; he is equally anomalous and assumes the form of a giant or titan and, as such, takes on a titanic and destructive role. It is with profound psychological and spiritual insight that Buddhism places the heaven of the Titans below the heaven of the humans, for the titanic aspect is not only an imbalance and destructive, but also takes man out of his central position. The Taoist artist must be fully human and his art neither renounces the world, nor is it immersed in the realm of the senses. It is an art which is "at once so human and so visionary" and has an "astonishing mixture of spirituality and naive joy … and with it a subtle sense of mystery"; it has a "noble joyousness" and "a refined joyousness".[14] No other religion has linked so closely art, mysticism, and laughter.

Calligraphy was always regarded as an art in China, the Chinese script being essentially pictorial and, like painting, it was done with a fine brush and so had a fluidity, grace, and flexibility impossible in the hard point of a pencil. It was also subject to the same immediacy as painting. Using a brush on silk, the strokes had to be quick, sure, and unhesitating, there was no second chance, no possibility of

Calligraphy attributed to Wang Hsien-chih (344-388), Eastern Chin dynasty

Three Passages of Calligraphy (detail), early T'ang tracing copy of Wang Hsi-chih (303-361)

[14] Ibid.

erasing, modifying, or painting over a mistake. Both were subject to the same immediacy as life itself; the movement, the choice, was irrevocable, there was no going back and each line had to be in correct relationship with the others. Both painting and calligraphy were usually in monochrome but commanded an immense variety of shades. There was a deceptive simplicity of style, a simplicity and spontaneity attained, as in *wu-wei*, by long years of practicing and a rigorous self-discipline. The light and shade also represent the *yin-yang* play of all the complementary opposites. Great artists were known by their calligraphy as much as by their paintings and both had to be spontaneous and rhythmic, but while painting could express the beauty of the subject, calligraphy relied only on its own beauty of form. Confucius said that "a man's character is apparent in every brush-stroke". The writing of the renowned calligraphist Wan Tsi Chih was said to be "as light as floating clouds and as vigorous as a startled dragon". Calligraphy also provided a link between painting and poetry. The calligraphist was already an artist and had mastered rhythm-with-movement, an essential element in poetry. An artist also frequently added a poem in a corner of his painting, expressing the same idea in the two media.

The artist-poet-musician and calligraphist could only be of the gentleman-scholar class, a class based solely on scholarship and not on birth. It was an intellectual aristocracy, but the intellectualism was not one-sided. The scholar was expected to be highly trained and proficient in both mind and body, and the art of archery was practiced to this end, requiring, as it does, physical fitness, keenness of eye, and quiet control of movement. He was also expected to perform his social and civic duties,

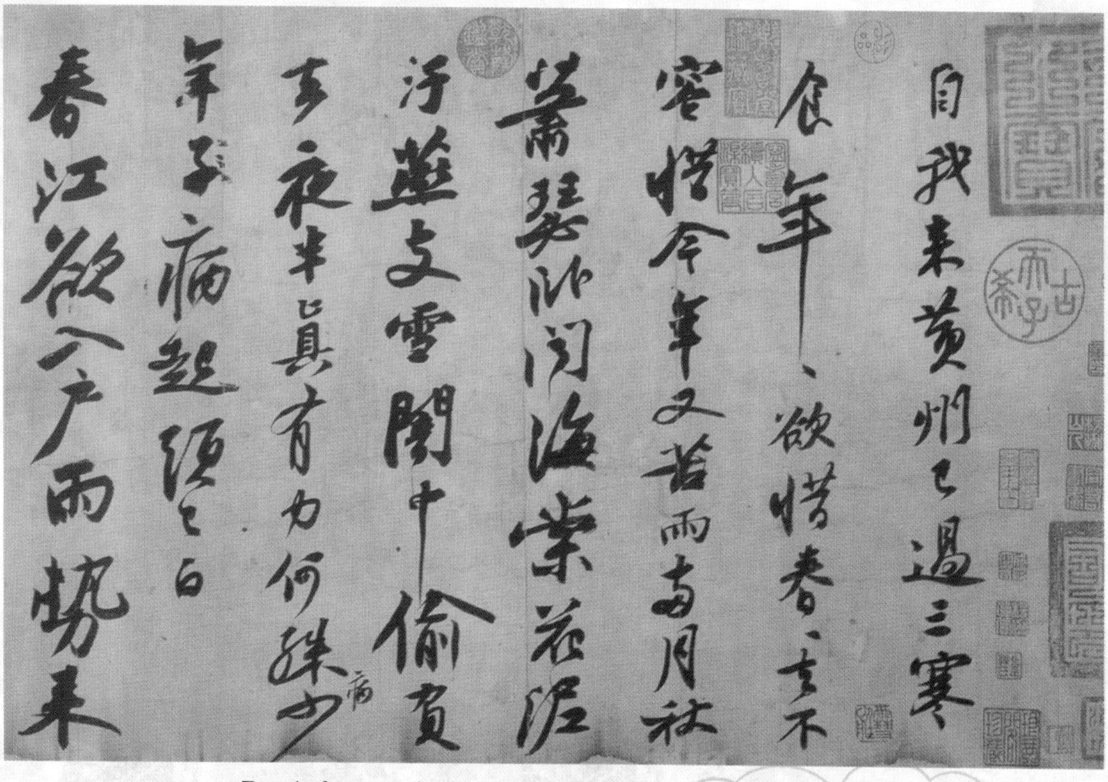

Detail of a piece of calligraphy by Mi Fu (1051-1107), Sung dynasty

though he sought solitude for his recreation and spiritual renewal, just as poets and artists went into the wild places to live in touch with nature. The scholar was also a man of integrity and was symbolized by the pine tree, standing straight and steadfast through all winds of adversity. All art, as with the work of the scholar, was necessarily intellectual rather than emotional, and poetry also contained little of the love element, compared with other subjects, and none of the passional. Chinese poems are short. There is an economy of words in which each one is used with telling effect. It was regarded as inefficiency in expression to use a profusion of words. The Western proliferation of words is defined by AE [George William Russell] as "inflated literary currency". There is no such inflation in Chinese poetry, which is aphoristic and concentrated in thought and expression. It has the compact quality of the diamond as compared with the diffuse and dull quality of quartz. A limit of twelve lines for a poem was set by convention for any candidate for the Imperial Examinations. There was no meticulous dotting of "i's" and crossing of "t's"; much was left unsaid so that, like the Void, it drew the reader or observer into actual participation and involved him directly. The stop-short and the sting-in-the-tail are frequently used.

All poetry is difficult to translate, but Chinese poetry particularly so as it is governed by rhyming rules which rhyme ideas as well as lines; also all words are monosyllables

Ma Yüan, *Mountain Path in the Spring*, Southern Sung dynasty

so the meter cannot be reproduced. For example, the monosyllables "Flower, middle, one, bottle, wine", form the opening line of one of Li Po's poems, translated into English as, "I take a bottle of wine and I go to drink it among the flowers". The poem is called "The little Fête".

I take a bottle of wine and I go to drink it among the flowers.
We are always three—counting my shadow and my friend the shimmering moon.
Happily the moon knows nothing of drinking, and my shadow is never thirsty.
When I sing, the moon listens to me in silence.
When I dance, my shadow dances too.
After all festivities the guests must depart;
This sadness I do not know.
When I go home, the moon goes with me and my shadow follows me.

Li Po has been called "the poet of heroic abandon" who laughed at life and advocated living it to the full. He was said to have drunk a hundred cups of wine before starting to compose poems. It should be pointed out, though, that the "cup" was about the size of a thimble, even tea cups were delicate and small. As Chamaileon, a disciple of Aristotle, said, large cups are a characteristic of barbarians!

From Wan Tsi, who was probably a contemporary of Chuang Tzu, comes an excellent example of the sting-in-the-tail poem.

On my flute of ebony I have played you the most beautiful air that I know,
But you have looked at the peonies and have not listened to me.
I have written you a poem in which I celebrated your beauty,
But you tore it up and threw the pieces on the lake,
Because, you said, the lake had no water lilies.
I would like to give you a wonderful sapphire,
Limpid and cold as a winter's night,
But I keep it that I may remember your heart.

Another is by Su Shih, who wrote a poem to celebrate the birth of his son.

Families, when a son is born,
Want it to be intelligent.
I, through intelligence,
Having wrecked my whole life,
Only hope the child will prove
Ignorant and stupid.
Then he will crown a tranquil life
By becoming a Cabinet Minister.

Much of the T'ang Taoist poetry was a landscape painting in words, such as Li Po's—

The travelers, listening to the sound of the zither . . .
Heard the rustling pines in myriad chasms,
The dying notes like falling frost on bells.
I had not noticed dusk come to the mountains,
Nor seen how deep the autumn clouds were darkened.

and Tu Fu, a contemporary of Li Po—

In limpid autumn nothing obscures my view;
On the horizon a light mist is rising,
A distant river melts into the sky,
A solitary city sinks in the milky mist.
A few leaves are falling, blown by the breeze;
The sun sets behind the curving hill.
How late the solitary crane returns!

It is twilight and the rooks are already
flocking to the forest.

While the vastness of the mountain scenes and landscapes in painting conveys the vision evoked by contemplation, poetry, by contrast, is often more intimate and homely. Painting is often an expression of the ineffable, poetry often the charm of the quiet and homely scene and, with music, it frequently expresses the social and convivial. Po Chu-i wrote—

Lined coat, warm cap, and easy felt slippers.
In the little tower, at the low window,
Sitting over a sunken brazier.
Body at rest, heart at peace; no need to rise early.
I wonder if the courtiers at the Western Capital know of these things or not?

and Wang An-shih, in his home, writes—

It is midnight; all is silent in the house; the water clock has stopped.
But I am unable to sleep because of the beauty of the trembling shapes
Of the spring flowers thrown by the moon upon the blind.

Drama, in China, was of a later development and had in it no element of the sacred. It was an entirely popular or court entertainment and was not the work of scholars. Actors were, with soldiers, an outcast class, and plays and novels were written in the colloquial or spoken language, while poetry, philosophy, and the classics were in the classical language of the scholars, a dead language to the public at large. No scholar admitted to knowing anything of the popular plays or novels.

Artefacts, on the other hand, the work of

Pitcher with phoenix head spout, Shan Hsi, end of Five Dynasties period, late 10th century

Nephrite jade vase, Han dynasty

Opposite: Monk Chü-jan (fl. 10th century), *Seeking after the Tao in Autumn Mountains*, Five Dynasties period

Perforated disk with two dragons and grain pattern, Warring States period

Pair of pendants carved in the shape of dragons, Han dynasty, 2nd century

the artist-craftsman, were symbolic in design and expressions of the craftsman's spiritual vision. He approached his work from a contemplative attitude. Chuang Tzu illustrates this with the story of the emperor's chief carpenter whose work "appeared to be of supernatural execution". The Prince of Lu asked him, "What mystery is there in your art?" "No mystery, Your Highness", replied Ch'ing, "and yet there is something. When I am about to make something I guard against any diminution of my power. I first reduce my mind to absolute quiescence. Three days in this condition, and I become oblivious to any fame to be acquired. Seven days, and I become unconscious of my four limbs and my physical frame. Then with no thought of the court present in my mind, my skill becomes concentrated and all disturbing elements from without are gone.... I bring my own native capacity into relation with that of the wood. What was suspected to be of supernatural execution in my work was due solely to this."[15] It is this putting of the

[15] *Chuang Tzu* XIX, trans. Giles.

Taoist stele dedicated to Lao Tzu, dated 572

native capacity into relation with the material used that is so important in Chinese carving of jade and the use of agate and crystal and in capturing the milky lunar light of the moonstone. The work is essentially a development of the potential in the medium and the sympathy between the artist and his material. There is also a deep appreciation of the "feeling" of the material and there are pieces of jade designed and kept entirely to be handled and felt. The surface is said to glow with the inner life and impart the symbolic qualities of the jade to the handler. The polish representing purity, its smoothness, benevolence; its compactness, strength and sureness of the intellect; angular, but not sharp, it is justice; hanging in beads, it is humility; its flaws, which are not concealed, but do not mar its beauty, are loyalty; its transparency is sincerity; it is mysterious and iridescent as the heavens and is formed of the mountains and the waters of the earth; the value of all men set upon it represents truth.

Sculpture seems to have played a comparatively insignificant part in China, with the exception of the vast figures used in the imperial tombs and the T'ang stelae, until the advent of Buddhism.

In architecture, the forms of buildings, whether pagodas, palaces, or private houses, were designed either to merge into the landscape, or to pick up and accentuate some outstanding beauty of scene and setting. The position of monasteries was chosen for natural beauty and the solitude of contemplation, but all buildings, as with all other branches of Chinese art, carried no weight of permanence or sense of solidarity, so that the transitory is suggested and all is an embodiment of the philosophy of the rhythm of the universe and its constant interactions. Metaphysics inspires art and art gives rise to metaphysics.

Mount Wu Tang in Hu-pei province, a sacred mountain in Taoism

Monastery on a cliff facing the peak of Mount T'ai, one of the "Five Sacred Mountains", Shan-tung province

Temple of Heaven, Beijing

Entrance to the Taoist Fo-shan Ancestral Temple, Kuang-tung province, Sung dynasty

10. SYMBOLISM

The symbol has within it the evocative power of the myth, so essential for the wellbeing of man's mental and spiritual life and health, so that, in the traditional East, art and symbolism were so closely bound as to be indistinguishable. "It is the business of art to grasp the primordial truth, to make the inaudible audible, to enunciate the primordial word, to reproduce the primordial images—or it is not art.... In other words, a real art is one of symbolic and significant representation; a representation of things that cannot be seen except by the intellect."[1]

In Taoist art there was nothing that was not symbolic and every symbol was a window on to a realm that is greater than the symbol itself and greater than the man who perceives it, and, with the myth, is only living and effective if it evokes a sense of the numinous and leads to a power beyond itself, beyond the obvious and the natural, that is to the supernatural. As Coleridge says, "A symbol ... always partakes of the Reality which it renders intelligible; and while it enunciates the whole, abides itself as a living part of that Unity of which it is representative"; and Carlyle might have been re-enunciating the *yin-yang* principle when he wrote that "in a symbol there is concealment but yet revelation, silence and speech acting together; the infinite blending with the finite."

The symbol which embodies Taoism, par excellence, is the dragon, and it not only symbolizes the religion but its reputed founder also. In one of the meetings between Lao Tzu and Confucius, probably invented by Chuang Tzu to carry his point, Confucius says, "I

[1] Andrae, quoted from Coomaraswamy's *Christian and Oriental Philosophy of Art*.

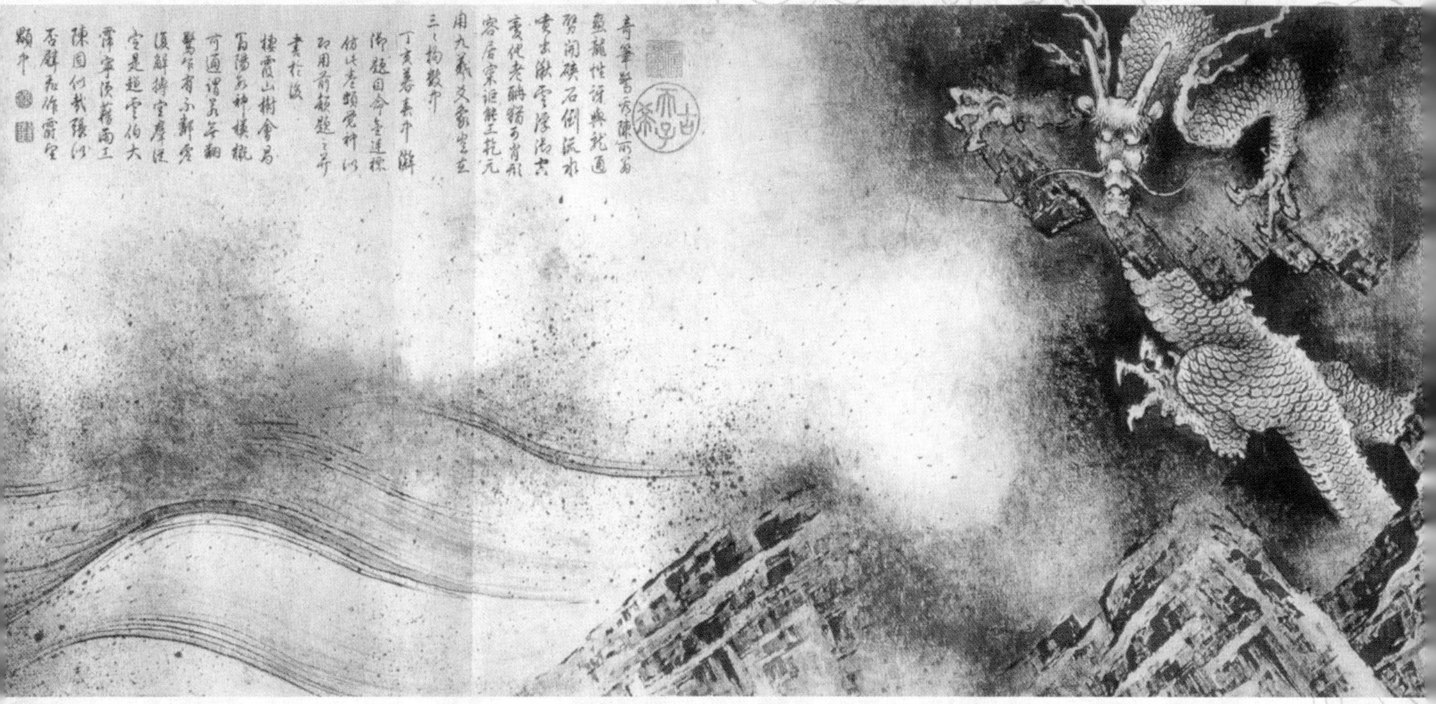

Ch'en Jung (active 1235-1262), *Nine Dragons*, Southern Sung dynasty, 1244

know birds can fly, fishes swim, and animals run. But the runner may be snared, the swimmer hooked, and the flyer shot by an arrow. But there is the dragon—I cannot tell how he mounts on the wind, through the clouds, and rises to Heaven. Today I have seen Lao Tzu. I can only compare him to the dragon."

The dragon and the phoenix represent the emperor and empress in all imperial art, but each is capable of embodying the cosmic unity of the *yin-yang* in itself. The *yang* dragon of the heavens can become the *yin* dragon of the waters, and the *yin* phoenix can become the *yang* vermilion bird of fire, each symbolizing the mystic powers of the *yin* and *yang* and resolving the opposites of fire and water, the two great creative elements. The phoenix, the *feng-huang*, is made up of various elements. It has the head of a cock, the back of a swallow, its eyes are the sun, its beak is the crescent moon, its wings are the wind, its tail represents trees and flowers, and its feet are the earth. It does not mature for three years and then it, too, has five colors, blue, yellow, red, white, and black which symbolize the cardinal virtues of uprightness, justice, honesty, benevolence, and fidelity. "Its color delights the eyes, its comb expresses righteousness, its tongue utters sincerity, its voice chants melody, its ears enjoy music, its heart conforms to regulations, its breast contains the treasures of literature and its spurs are powerful against transgressors." It also was only seen in auspicious times and its appearance meant peace and benevolent rule and the advent of a great sage, while a pair of phoenixes denoted a combination of emperor and sage and was seen in the reigns of Yao, Shun, and Huang Ti.

The magnificent dragon robes, which the emperors wore at the solstice sacrifices, symbolically clothed them in the universe and displayed all the cosmic symbols of heaven, earth and the waters, the mountains and clouds, and the waves of the ocean. The glory of these

Manchu man's court robe, 18th century

robes was not a vain adornment of the male, nor to add consequence and pomp to man and ceremony, but to serve as a constant reminder of man's place in the universe, to recall the spiritual powers controlling heaven and earth, and to keep in mind the hierarchic order of things celestial and terrestrial, to which man must conform on its various levels and according to his varying capacities. The emperor, as the Son of Heaven, or the Great Light, was the supreme spiritual as well as temporal power and was thus clothed in the powers of the universe and the symbol of perfection.

The "dragon with the ball" has given rise to endless speculation as to its symbolism. Some suggest that it is the dragon as rain-bringer, belching out thunder, or trying to capture and swallow the ball, while de Visser offers the theory that the ball is the moon which the dragon, as clouds, would approach and swallow; but this would equally apply to the sun. All these are rain symbols with which the dragon was connected, but, in Chinese, the ball is usually called the "precious pearl" or the "flaming pearl" or the "pearl of effulgence"—a lunar symbol—and Tu Fu writes of the black dragon "breathing out pearls looming out of the darkness". The pearl is also "the jewel which grants desires", so it would seem that while the dragon is the rain-bringer and symbol of the powers of the waters on the material level, he is, as in almost universal symbolism, also the guardian of treasures, and, as master of the deep, guards the pearl of per-

One of the enameled terracotta panels on either side of the gate of the Hall of Spiritual Cultivation, Beijing

fection which on the spiritual level represents enlightenment.

The dragon has endless powers of transformation, from the largest to the smallest form and is the embodiment of the powers of change in nature and the life of man and of the forces of the eternal flux. Of him Okakura writes, "He is the spirit of change, therefore of life itself. Hidden in the caves of inaccessible mountains or coiled in the unfathomable depth of the sea, he awaits the time when he slowly rouses himself to activity. He unfolds himself in the storm clouds, he washes his mane in the blackness of the seething whirlpools. His claws are forks of lightning; his scales begin to glisten in the bark of rain-swept pine trees. His voice is heard in the hurricane which, scattering the withered leaves of the forest, quickens a new spring…".

The perfect rhythm of the form of the dragon epitomizes all that is contained in Taoist mysticism and its art. It is the ultimate mystery, hiding itself in clouds, on mountain tops, and in deep places, it thus symbolizes wisdom itself—the Tao.

In alchemy, the fiery aspect of the dragon, in contrast to his rain-bringing aspect, is the power of transmuting and transcending the earthly state in burning out the dross to attain spiritual freedom and realization.

In scholarship the "dragon's gate" is the great testing place, the barrier that must be surmounted. The carp symbolizes ordinary man who, once he has "leaped the dragon's

Ma Yüan, *Waves*, Southern Sung dynasty

gate", becomes, on the lower level, one who has achieved the heights of the Imperial Examinations in the classics, or, on the higher level, has attained enlightenment. The carp is the symbol of perseverance, courage, and determination on the way to attaining the powers symbolized by the dragon.

Next to the dragon, and connected with it, water is the most frequently employed symbol in Taoism. It is the strength in apparent weakness, the fluidity of life, and also symbolic of the state of coolness of judgment, acceptance, and passionlessness, as opposed to the heat of argument, the friction of opposition, and the emotion of desire. Water fertilizes, refreshes, and purifies and is symbolic of gentle persuasion in government of the state and in the individual. It occupies the lowest position, yet is the most powerful of forces. "The highest goodness is like water. Water is beneficent to all things but does not contend. It stays in places which others despise. Therefore it is near Tao." "The weakest things in the world can overmatch the strongest things in the world. Nothing in the world can be compared to water for its weak and yielding nature; yet in attacking the hard and the strong nothing proves better than it. For there is no alternative to it. The weak can overcome the strong and the yielding can overcome the hard. This all the world knows but does not practice."[2] This is, again, the doctrine of *wu-wei* and non-violence. Water may be weak, pliable, fluid, but its action is not one of running away from an obstacle. On the contrary it gives at the point of resistance, envelops the object and passes on beyond it. Ultimately it will wear down the hardest rock. Water is a more telling symbol than land. Crossing vast expanses of water or fast-flowing torrents is more awe-inspiring

[2] *Tao Te Ching* LXXVIII, trans. Ch'u Ta-kao.

Opposite: Fan K'uan (fl. 990-1030), *Mountain Landscape*, Northern Sung dynasty

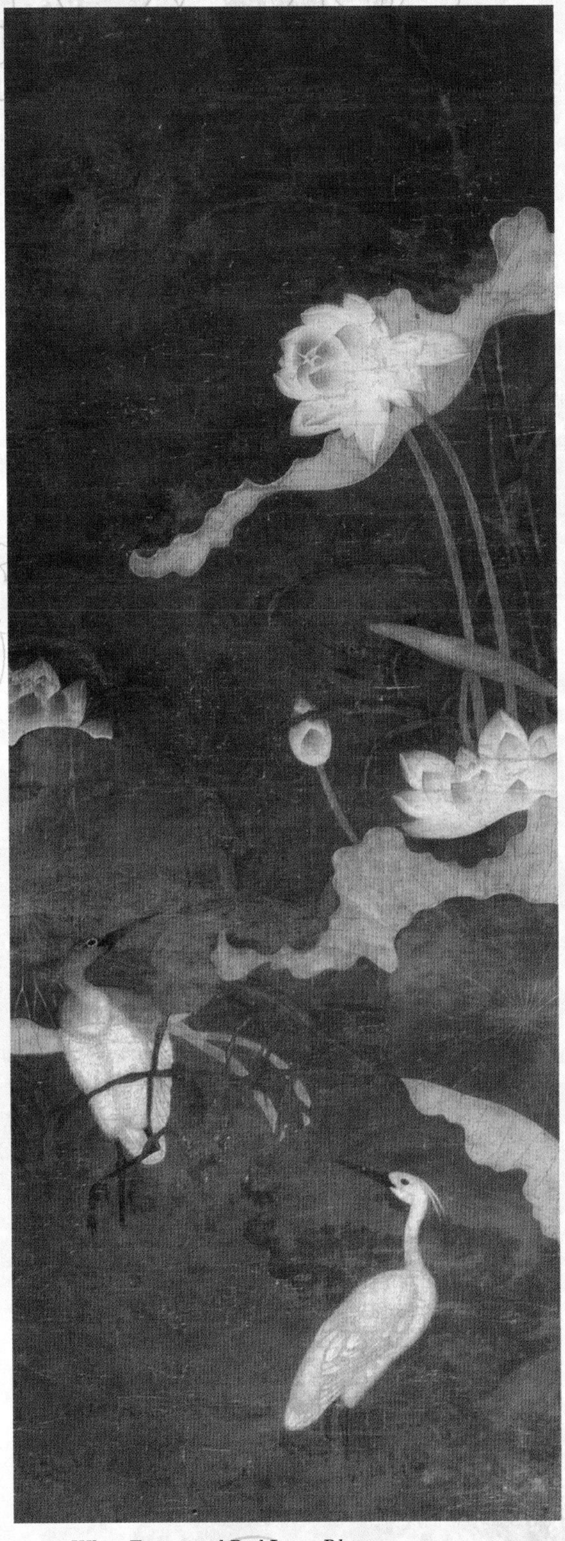

White Egrets and Red Lotus Blossoms, anonymous,
Yüan dynasty, late 13th-early 14th century

and dangerous; there is less chance of finding a way round it, the challenge has to be met directly, hence all the symbolism of the "rivers of life" and crossing the river to get to the other side, which is, again, attaining the state of enlightenment. The wise man, in crossing the river, does not exhaust his strength in violently opposing the current, nor does he allow himself to be washed away by it, but, utilizing the currents as they come, he gives way here and makes way there, until, with the minimum of effort and the maximum use of the natural, he attains.

Perfection and enlightenment are also symbolized by the lotus, which, like the dragon and phoenix, contains in itself a balance of the *yin-yang* qualities. Germinating in the darkness of the mud, it grows up through the opaque waters to bloom in the air in the full light of the sun. Its roots symbolize indissolubility, its stem the umbilical cord of life, and its flowering is expansion and realization in the realm of light. Thus it represents the whole growth, potentialities, and spiritual development of man in the world. On the feminine *yin* side it is the emblem of Kwan-yin (as the lotus, or lily, is the attribute of all Queens of Heaven or Great Mothers) and symbolizes feminine beauty, purity, and perfection. It is also the symbol of past, present, and future as the same plant bears buds, flowers, and seeds at one time. As it contains both the *yin* and *yang* powers of water and light, it is a totality; as self-created, self-existent, it is the Tao.

Like the phoenix (*feng-huang*), the *ky-lin* shows the *yin-yang* not as two creatures in opposition but as blended into a unity. The *ky-lin*, the *ky* being the *yang* and the *lin* the *yin*, is sometimes called the unicorn and would, as such, be wholly feminine *yin* since the feminine aspect is usually attached to the lunar

Opposite: *Kwan-yin with Moon and Water*, detail of a painting from Tun-huang, Kansu province, anonymous, dated 943

Feng-huang (phoenix) sculpture at the Summer Palace, Beijing

unicorn; in which case the animal is referred to as the *lin* and symbolizes gentleness, purity, goodwill, and benevolence. If it is not depicted as a unicorn it is a composite creature with the head of a dragon, with a single horn, the mane of a lion, the body of a stag, and the tail of an ox. It can also be represented as a dragon-deer mixture, in which case it returns to the *yin-yang* combination. It has five symbolic colors, red, green, violet, yellow, and blue; its body, with its horn, is twelve feet high and is composed of the five elements. Like the *feng-huang*, with which it is always associated, it is never anything but an auspicious omen and appears only in the reign of an emperor-sage, or to announce the birth of a sage. A *ky-lin* was said to have appeared to the mother of Confucius, knelt before her, and presented her with a piece of jade, which is masculine-*yang*, thus announcing the birth of a world-famous son. Late in his life when a *ky-lin*, unrecognized for what it was, was shot by some hunters in the Imperial Park, Con-

Ky-lin, Han dynasty

Goddess of the Sky Riding a Phoenix, attributed to Chang Seng-yu (active 500-550), Six Dynasties period

fucius wept for the *ky-lin* and recognized in its death the omen of the end of his work and life. As the creature was a symbol of a wise king or great statesman, an exceptionally clever child was called "a son of a *ky-lin*", and to "ride a *ky-lin*" was to rise to fame. In Chinese art great sages and immortals are represented as mounted on a *ky-lin*, this denoting their exceptional qualities. The *ky-lin* and phoenix both have characters of great gentleness, the former never crushes any living thing with its feet and never strikes with its horn, which symbolizes benevolence. Only having one horn symbolizes the unity of the world under one great ruler. The phoenix does not live by injuring anything and eats only seed and drinks heavenly dew.

As is to be expected of a nation which took delight in every aspect of nature and in life itself, all flowers played a significant part in Chinese symbolism, though universally in symbolism plants, flowers, and trees take a highly important place. In every part of the world the tree not only represents resurrec-

Ma Yüan, *Immortal Riding a Dragon*, Southern Sung dynasty, early 13th century

Peonies, anonymous, Sung dynasty

tion, but its form depicts diversity in unity; its manifold branches rise from one root and are again one in the potentiality of the seed in the fruit of those branches. In their dying and resurrection, trees and flowers are equated with the cyclic force of life and death and rebirth and so are closely associated with the feminine, lunar power. It is not merely their attractiveness and beauty which singles them out as emblems of feminine charm and loveliness, but the deep-rooted symbolism of the Great Mother, the Queen of Heaven, the essence of feminine perfection and power. As she stands for the changing world of manifestation, for birth, death, and rebirth, for the moon which dies and is born again, so all plant life is an obvious analogy of transitoriness, fragility, and quick-passing life; but it also depicts, in the tree, the quality of strength and protectiveness and the sheltering aspect of the feminine principle. In China the Queen of Heaven was above all Kwan-yin, "she who was born of the lotus", "she who hears the cry of the world". She embodies only the aspect of compassion, loving wisdom, and inspiration of the Great Mother and none of her fierce, dark qualities. Later, under the influence of Buddhism, she developed Buddhist characteristics and was equated with Avalokitesvara, but in Taoism she is associated with the Tao as the Mother of All Things.

Few flowers are *yang*, notable exceptions being the peony, a royal flower, supposed to be untouched by any insect but the bee, and depicting light and masculinity, glory and riches, and the lotus which can be *yang* or *yin* according to whether it is portraying solar light or the lunar power of the waters.

The flower, by its cup-like shape, is a natural symbol for the open, receptive, and passive *yin*, and in marriage symbolism and decorations flowers represent the woman, while the horse and lion, as speed and strength, represent the man. In both poetry and painting, flowers are frequently connected with the moon, which shares the transience of flowers. Its mysterious light, striking through the delicate branches of flowering trees, or suffusing a landscape of mountains, rivers, lakes, and willows, brings to life a world of shadows and solitude, fit setting and subject for the poet, artist, or sage. The willow itself is a symbol of artistic ability and, with the pine, is the tree which, except for the bamboo, appears most frequently in Chinese art. The pine is allied to the sun and is masculine strength, longevity, great vitality, and strong will; as being both solar and evergreen it represents immortality and eternal existence. The willow, in contrast, is *yin*, lunar, pliable, graceful, and charming and is an emblem of Kwan-yin, who sprinkles the waters of life with a willow branch. Here again is a Taoist example of strength-in-weakness and weakness-in-strength, for the weakness of the strong pine is that, standing

Ma Yüan, *Discussing Tao Under the Pines*, Southern Sung dynasty, early 13th century

Lake Retreat Among Willow Trees, anonymous, Southern Sung dynasty, c. 1200-1250

erect and unyielding in a storm, it is lashed and broken by the winds; holding its boughs out rigidly in snow, they crack under the weight. The weak willow bends before the storm, moves its branches with it, and survives; its branches droop under the weight of snow, which slides off and the boughs spring back to life again.

The bamboo, however, combines both qualities of erectness and pliability. It is the tree, *par excellence*, of the Chinese painter, philosopher, and poet. Whole books have been written on the art of painting bamboo and artists have spent their entire lives in perfecting the art; it was one of the greatest artistic achievements of the T'ang dynasty under Taoism. Sages, poets, and artists all dwelt, when possible, in the bamboo forests where the rustle of the leaves in the breeze is the murmur of the voice of remote places, of mountain gorges and deep groves; the voice of the silence, wisdom herself. The bamboo is all the qualities of the soul of man and of nature epitomized. Seldom painted in other than black and white, throwing into relief darkness and light, expressing power and delicacy, it is the *yin-yang* symbol of the universe. It is the embodiment of dignity and nobility; the austerity of its form is wisdom and the severe simplicity of abstract thought. It is the fine character which bends before the storm but does not break; it is the scholar-gentleman who is upright in bearing but has an inner "emptiness" and humility; it is the perfect ruler, austere, virtuous, dignified, and wise; it is gracefulness, fastidiousness, constancy, and yielding but enduring strength.

In contrast to the qualities of strength in the bamboo, pine, and willow, the fragile and evanescent appearance of the convolvulus is a natural symbol of transitoriness, the shortness of life, quick glory, and decline and premature death, but it is maintained that, although it lives only for an hour of its "morning glory", it in no way differs at heart from the pine which lives a thousand years. It is a frequently reiterated belief in Taoist philosophy that each living thing plays its allotted part in the universe and no greater value attaches to the long life of the pine than to the brief beauty of the convolvulus, and it is said of the "morning glory" that to live happily, having conformed to its true nature, is to die happy in the evening, having enjoyed the full glory of the sun and expressed perfection of beauty. It knows no envy of the pine, each fulfilling its own destiny.

Chuang Tzu often refers to Lieh Tzu, of whom little is known. Some have even gone so far as to suggest that he was not a real person but a figment of Chuang Tzu's mind, created to put over a different point of view, accentuate some different aspect, or introduce a difference in style (an exercise which was

Li K'an (1245-1320), *Peace in the Four Seasons*, Yüan dynasty

part of the tests of the Imperial Examinations), but authorities differ and many think that Lieh Tzu, or Lieh Yu-kuo, shows an unmistakable style of his own. It is less sparkling but more kindly than that of Chuang Tzu; both use typically Chinese methods of legend and allegory to convey their teachings, but one of the chief characteristics of Lieh Tzu's writing is that he expresses, throughout, the early, primordial and paradisal state in which the sages of old lived with animals, spoke their language, and shared with them a perfect understanding, knowing that there is "no wide gulf between any living species" and none has the right to batten on the other. It is not surprising, then, that animals as well as flowers and trees are employed in sacred symbolism and in the *yin-yang* philosophy of life. The Dragon, Phoenix, and *Ky-lin*, with the Tortoise, are called the "Four Spiritually Endowed" or Sacred Animals. Three of these "animals" are fabulous, composite creatures uniting in themselves both the *yin* and *yang*. The Tortoise is the only natural animal among them, but all are symbols of spiritual power as well as of cosmic forces and the elements. The three composite creatures all represent also the androgyne. Again, in the West, the figure of the androgyne is anthropomorphic, either as a male-female figure, or the somewhat crude bearded goddess, or the young, effeminate, and beautiful Dying God and the masculine hunting goddesses or nymphs; in Taoism the fabulous creatures played this part.

As the power of the waters the Tortoise is the beginning of creation. His color is black as representative of primordial chaos, night, and the northern regions and, as in other traditions, notably Hindu, Egyptian, and South American, he is portrayed as a support for the world. Known as "The Black Warrior" and symbolizing endurance and strength, the Tortoise appeared with the Dragon on the banners of the army since both creatures survive a fight; the Dragon cannot crush the Tortoise and the Tortoise cannot reach the Dragon.

The Tiger, in China, took the place of the lion as King of the Beasts and "Lord of the Earth and land animals", the lion being introduced later with Buddhism, but here Buddhism and Taoism seem to have influenced

Tortoise entwined with a snake, stone rubbing after Wu Tao-tzu, renowned painter of the T'ang dynasty

each other very little, for the tiger remained an important animal in Taoist symbolism while, for the Buddhist, he was one of the "Three Senseless Creatures" as typifying anger, with the monkey as grasping greed, and the deer as love-sickness. Of the seasons, the tiger represents autumn, the time of fierce storms and raging winds and the tiger roaring through the forests looking for a mate. He is then *yang* as strength, fierceness, and destructive power, and denotes military prowess and courage and was the emblem of officers of the Fourth

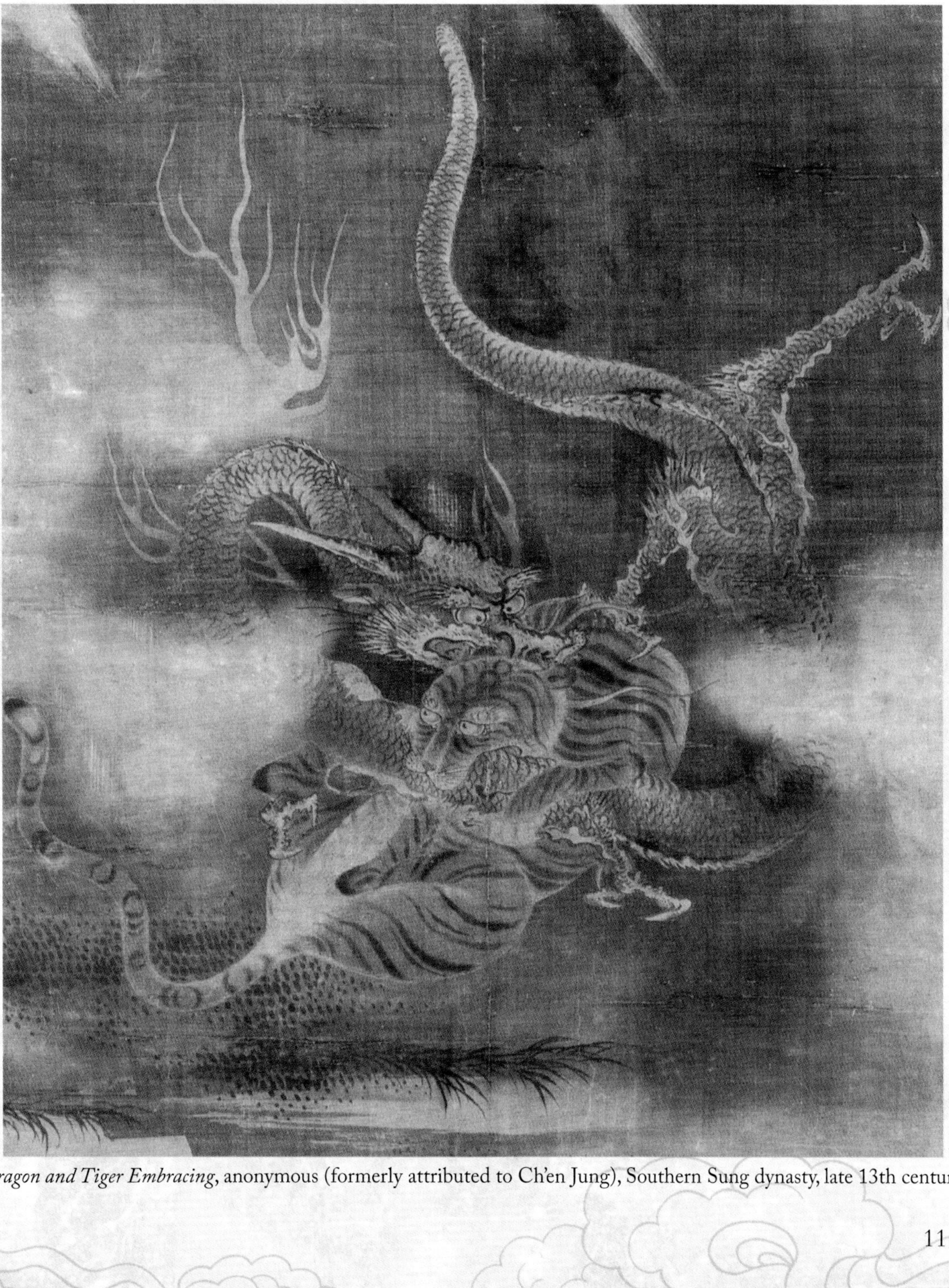

Dragon and Tiger Embracing, anonymous (formerly attributed to Ch'en Jung), Southern Sung dynasty, late 13th century

Class; but when he appears in conflict with the dragon, the tiger becomes *yin*, the Earth, and matter opposing the celestial forces of the spirit. The White Tiger is always *yin* and, being able to see in the dark, it is lunar and chthonic and signifies the region of the West, always associated with death. He is a messenger of the gods and is ridden by gods, immortals, and magicians. As with the underworld Pluto, the chthonic tiger also represents wealth and is a guardian of the treasure chests; the god of wealth rides on the tiger who is also the emblem of gamblers and is invoked by them.

Ch'en Yüeh Hsi, *The Taoist Immortal Ma Ku with a Crane and Flower Basket*, Yüan dynasty, 14th century

While the White Tiger is *yin* and lunar, the other messenger of the gods, the Crane, "The Patriarch of the Feathered Tribes", is entirely *yang* and solar and is usually associated with the pine tree. The pure white crane lives in the Isles of the Blest and the Western Paradise. As pure white it is connected with the paradisial state of innocence and purity and as a bird it symbolizes transcendence, the celestial powers and the soul which can fly from the body. In art it frequently accompanies great rulers, scholars, or Taoist sages. In particular it is the emblem of one of the Eight Taoist Genii, or Immortals, who symbolize the various facets of Taoism. Li T'ieh-kuai is always depicted as a beggar with a crutch and gourd and a crane at his feet. As a sage he was able to leave his body and travel in the realms of spirit at will, but once he was away from his body for so long that when he got back he found that it had been buried, so, looking round for another body to use, he saw that of a beggar who had just died by the roadside; he got into it and in it spent the rest of his mortal life. Seeing him accompanied by a crane is enough to convey to the knowledgeable that this would be no ordinary beggar who had with him a companion of the gods. When he is portrayed in art, jade carving, or porcelain figures, he has a look of inward serenity combined with a puckish humor which is only enhanced by the mean exterior. He also represents the Taoist love of laughing at appearances and the fact that the outward form is illusory and inner greatness is often hidden from the undiscerning.

Lu Chih (1496-1576), *Chuang Tzu Dreaming of a Butterfly*, Ming dynasty, mid 16th century

Chuang Tzu constantly employs bird and animal symbolism, as when, illustrating the doctrine of naturalness and Original Simplicity, he puts into the mouth of Lao Tzu, supposed to be talking to Confucius who is arguing for conventional morality, the words: "All this talk of charity and duty to one's neighbor drives me nearly crazy. Sir, strive to keep the world in its original simplicity and, as the wind blows wheresoever it listeth, so let virtue establish itself. Wherefore this undue energy, as though searching for a fugitive with a big drum? The swan is white without a daily bath, the raven is black without daily coloring itself. The original simplicity of black and white are beyond the reach of argument. The vista of fame and reputation are hardly worth enlarging. When the pond dries up and the fish are left upon dry ground, to moisten them with the breath or damp them with a little spittle is not to be compared with leaving them as at first in their native waters."[3]

The butterfly, with its amazing metamorphosis from the clumsy and mundane caterpillar, through complete dissolution, to the glorious celestial winged creature, is a universal symbol of the soul, rebirth, and immortality. It is with these associations that Chuang Tzu uses it in his famous allegory of the illusory and dream quality of the world. "Once upon a time Chuang Tzu dreamed that he was a butterfly, a butterfly flying about and enjoying itself. It did not know it was Chuang Tzu. Suddenly he awoke and veritably was Chuang Tzu again. We do not know whether it was Chuang Tzu dreaming that he was a butterfly, or whether it was a butterfly dreaming it was Chuang Tzu."[4] Lieh Tzu uses the same type of parable when he writes of the old slave em-

[3] *Chuang Tzu*, trans. Legge.

[4] *Chuang Tzu* II, trans. Fung Yu-lan.

ployed by a wealthy master who worked his servants unmercifully. Each night the old man dreamed he was a king and enjoyed pleasures and palaces, ease and the good things of life, while each night his master dreamed he was a slave, ill-treated, ill-fed and harshly used, and suffering nights of agony; so, "if you want to distinguish between waking and dreaming, only the Yellow Emperor or Confucius could help you, but both these sages are dead." But Chuang Tzu says: "By and by comes the great awakening, and then we shall find out that life itself is a great dream. All the while fools think they are awake; that they know, and with nice discriminations they make distinctions between princes and grooms. How stupid! Confucius and you are both a dream. When I say you are a dream, I am also a dream. This saying is called a paradox."[5]

The chief beast of burden in ancient China was the water buffalo, an ungainly, strong, extremely intransigent and often fierce animal. These characteristics made him a fitting symbol of man's unregenerate nature and the sage riding a buffalo depicts the turbulent nature calmed and overcome by the perfection of the sage. Lao Tzu is frequently portrayed riding on a buffalo and legend has it that it was on a green buffalo that he rode out of this life. When he had stopped at the Western Pass, and, at the request of the Warden of the Pass, had written the *Tao Tê Ching*, and was ready to pass on, a green buffalo, saddled and bridled, presented itself before the hermitage where the old philosopher was living among the birds and beasts of the forest, and kneeled in front of the Sage who mounted on its back and was carried off at a gallop through the clouds and disappeared into the West.

The buffalo also appears in the Taoist-Buddhist series of symbolic pictures known as the "Ten Herding Pictures". At first the animal is painted as all black and is wild, uncaught, and totally undisciplined. Then he is caught, tethered, and the taming begins; later he is put into harness, but still cannot be allowed free. As the training goes on the animal becomes wholly docile and is then allowed to

Chang Lu (c. 1464-1538), *Lao Tzu on an Ox*, Ming dynasty, early-mid 16th century

[5] Ibid.

The Ox-Herding Sequence (detail), by the Japanese Zen monk Shubun (active c. 1423-1460): *Top left to right*: *Catching the Ox*; *Coming Home on the Ox's Back*; *Herding the Ox*; *Bottom left to right*: *Searching for the Ox*; *The Ox Forgotten, Leaving the Man Alone*; *The Ox and the Man Both Gone out of Sight*

wander freely and follows the herding-boy home; both can now enjoy themselves at leisure without giving thought to the other. In each successive picture the black buffalo gradually becomes whiter until, by the eighth picture, he is all white and the stars of the plough begin to appear in the sky. In the ninth picture the animal has disappeared altogether and the plough is complete in its stars in the sky, until, finally, the last picture is nothing but an empty circle, "both the man and the animal have disappeared, no traces are left, the bright moonlight is empty and shadowless with all the ten thousand things in it. If anyone should ask the meaning of this, behold the lilies of the field and their fresh, sweet-scented verdure."

Chief among the purely *yang* creatures are the Crane, Peacock, Cock, White Heron, and Falcon. The Falcon, though used as a symbol of bravery and courage, is a killer and belongs to the warrior class, which was always despised in traditional China, and so the bird was seldom portrayed in art and was stigmatized in poetry as its "sole delight is to kill and steal". The White Heron was always paired with the Black Crow as *yang* and *yin*. The heron, in Buddhism, takes on much of the symbolism of the crane in Taoism, and while the crane and pine are depicted together, the heron accompanies the willow in art and poetry. Strangely, though, the three-legged crow becomes solar and lives in the sun, but some query whether the "red" crow should not be the cock (stylized creatures can be easily confused), a purely solar bird, associated with the dawn, the disperser of clouds and darkness. Figures of the cock or crane were often seen on the roofs of houses where they warded off the powers of evil. Three-legged birds or animals represent either the rising, noon-day, and setting sun or, as in the case of lunar animals such as the three-legged toad or hare in the moon, the three phases of the moon. The Peacock is often represented as the King of Birds with the Peony as King of Flowers; it is the spirit of fire, the "Confucian Bird", and the Peacock feather was an imperial award for faithful service.

The dog can be *yin* or *yang*; it is the latter as the Celestial Dog who helps to drive

Left: *Hawk on a Pine Tree*, anonymous, Yüan dynasty, late 14th century
Right: *Cranes and Pine Tree*, Ch'ing dynasty, 18th century

Lü Chi (fl. c. 1477-1497), *Apricot Blossoms and Peacocks*, Ming dynasty

Emperor Hui-tsung (1082-1135), *Auspicious Cranes*, Sung dynasty

off evil spirits, but it is *yin* as guardian of the night hours. The fox, on the other hand, is wholly *yin* as nocturnal. It is magical, capable of endless transformations, its favorite guise being that of a beautiful maiden who lures would-be scholars away from their books. The fox-maiden is a laughing girl with the amoral qualities of the fairy world and can be cruel, teasing, or kind; sometimes she is even a good influence, as was the case of the fox-maiden who appeared to a student who promptly fell in love with her: She only allowed him to see her form in a mirror which could be found only in his books; if he neglected his work she appeared to cry, when he studied hard she was laughing and happy. This kept him working assiduously for three years until he passed the examinations with distinction. Happy in his triumph, he went to the mirror and saw his lady-love reflecting his happiness, whereupon she stepped out of the mirror to stand beside him and become his bride.

Some of the finest work in Chinese art went into the making of mirrors, usually of bronze, silver, or some other highly polished metal, smooth on one side and on the reverse symbolic designs of a religious, traditional, or cosmological significance. The mirror had the power of dispersing evil, for, once it is forced to see itself as it is, it bursts asunder at the horror of the sight: "when evil recognizes itself it destroys itself".

The symbolism of the mirror is bound up with sincerity on the lower and social plane, a quality which was pre-eminently valued, and on the spiritual plane as reflecting man's true nature. Like life, it will give back precisely what is given. It is the symbol of the Sage whose mind is a mirror: "The mind of the perfect man is like a mirror. It does not move with things, nor does it anticipate them. It responds to things, but does not retain them. Therefore the Sage is able to deal successfully with things, but is not affected."[6] It is both the reflection of the manifest, temporal world and of intelligence, of light, of the supreme principle, the Tao. Chu-hsi says, "We need not talk of empty and far away things; if we would know the reality of Tao we must seek it within our own nature. Each has within him the principle of right; this we call the Tao, the Way." But, "Tao is more than the way. It is the way and the way-goer. It is the eternal road, along it all beings and things walk; but no being made it, for it is being itself; it is everything and nothing and the cause and effect of all. All things originate from Tao, conform to Tao, and to Tao they at last return."[7]

Astronomical bronze mirror, early Eastern Han dynasty, 1st century

[6] Ibid., VII.

[7] R. K. Douglas, *Confucianism and Taoism* (published by S.P.C.K.).

11. THE TAOIST GARDEN

The development of the typical Chinese garden with its full *yin-yang* symbolism was essentially Taoist in origin. The Han Emperors had earlier created vast artificial landscapes or parks with mountains, ravines, forests, rivers, lakes, and open spaces to provide a habitat for hordes of game for hunting, but during the time of the Six Dynasties and the T'ang, when Taoism prevailed, there developed the quiet intimacy of the Taoist garden, intended to reflect heaven on earth. It became a symbol of Paradise where all life was protected and sheltered. The park had been given over to the grandiose, the artificial, extravagant, and luxurious, to the hunter and aggressor; the Taoist garden was a place of naturalness and simplicity, a haven for the sage, scholar, and nature lover.

Both landscape painting and garden-making owe their development to the Taoist philosophers who derived their inspiration from Nature as the Mother of All Things, the womb of life, eternal renewal, with her rhythms and moods. What was said of the painting of a landscape applied equally to the creation of a garden: "Chinese painters intuitively felt these same forms to be the visible, material manifestations of a higher all-embracing Reality; the Word made—not flesh—but Living Nature."[1] Or: "The Sages cherish the Tao within them, while they respond to the objective world.... As to landscapes, they both have material existence and reach to the realms of the Spirit.... The virtuous follow the Tao by spiritual insight and the wise take the same approach. Landscapes capture the Tao by their forms and the virtuous take pleasure in them. Is this not almost the same thing? .... The Divine Spirit is infinite, yet it dwells in forms and inspires likeness, and thus truth enters into forms and signs."[2] But while landscapes portrayed the vastness and grandeur of Nature, the garden revealed her intimate aspect.

All forms of art are the outward and visible expression of *Ch'i*, the Cosmic Breath or Energy, with which all creation must be in accord, whether it be painting, poetry, music, or the creation of a garden. Indeed, all these arts developed side by side, for the Chinese scholar was expected to be capable of interpreting the same inspiration in all three arts together and the place of both their inspiration and expression was most usually the garden, this term being applied also to the rural retreat of a sage or hermit where in some remote and beautiful scenery a hut had been built and round it trees planted. In a well-designed garden it should be difficult to distinguish between the work of man and Nature. One should "borrow scenery from Nature" and the ideal place was "among trees in the mountains". Wherever it was the garden was a place of quiet, meditation, and communion with Nature, whether in

[1] Michael Sullivan, *The Birth of Landscape Painting in China*, Routledge & Kegan Paul, 1962.

[2] From the *Hua shan-shui hsü*. Preface to painting by Tsung Ping.

Wen Cheng-ming (1470-1559), *View of the Humble Administrator's Gardens*, Ming dynasty

wild scenery beside a waterfall, or a trickling stream, or in a bamboo grove, or the courtyard of a city dwelling.

The garden is "the natural home of man" and house and garden were situated according to *feng-shui* (wind and water) influences in harmony with the currents of *Ch'i*; these were held in balance in both the house and garden, as in Nature, by the *yin-yang* forces. The *yin* lunar and *yang* solar powers were represented by the *yin* valleys and waters and the *yang* mountains and sky with all their endless *yang* and *yin* qualities such as sunshine and shadow, height and depth, heat and cold.

However small the space utilized the garden was never laid out as a flat expanse from which all could be viewed at once. This removal of any definite boundary made for succession, expansion, rhythm, and a sense of unlimited time and space. The garden, like Nature, is ever-changing, a place of light and shade with a life-breath (*Ch'i yün*) which is in harmony with the rhythms of the seasons and their contrasts in weather. Irregularity of line also suggests movement and life. "Everything that is ruled and symmetrical is alien to free nature."[3] Or, as it has been said: "The awareness of change, the interaction symbolized by the *yin-yang* theory, has caused Chinese gardeners to seek irregular and unexpected features which appeal more to the imagination than to the reasoning faculty of the beholder. There were certain rules and principles for gardening, but these did not lead to any con-

[3] From the *Yüan Yeh*, a Ming treatise on gardening.

Pavilion and zig-zag bridge in a garden, Kuang-tung province

formity. The basic elements were the same for landscape painting, *shan shui* or 'mountain and water'."[4] This "mountain and water" might be imposing scenery or simply a pond and rocks. The smallest space could be converted into an effect of depth, infinite extension, and mysterious distance; groves, rockeries, bushes, winding paths, all helped to lure on beyond the immediate scene. As Rowley says of Western and Chinese art: "We restrict space to a single vista as though seen through an open door; they suggest the unlimited space of nature as though they had stepped through that open door."[5]

[4] Yang Yap & A. Cotterell, *The Early Civilization of China.*

[5] *Principles of Chinese Painting*, Princeton, 1947.

The entire garden must be considered in association and relationship with all things in Nature. Chang Ch'ao says: "Planting flowers serves to invite butterflies, piling up rocks serves to invite the clouds, planting pine trees serves to invite the wind … planting banana trees serves to invite the rain and planting willow trees serves to invite the cicada." These are all traditional symbolic associations.

In the past in China, though man was the mediator between Heaven and Earth, he was not the measure of the universe; his place was simply to maintain the balance and harmony between the *yin* and the *yang*. It was Nature which was the Whole, and controlling cosmic power. The garden helped man in his work of maintaining harmony; it also had

The Little Flying Rainbow Bridge in the Distant Fragrance Hall, Humble Administrator's Garden, Su-chou, Chiang-su province

an ethical significance and influence. According to Ch'ien Lung it had "a refreshing effect upon the mind and regulated the feelings", preventing man from becoming "engrossed in sensual pleasures and losing strength of will". Its pleasures were simple, natural, and spiritual. A Suchou poet wrote of the garden: "One should enter it in a peaceful and receptive mood; one should use one's observation to note the plan and pattern of the garden, for the different parts have not been arbitrarily assembled, but carefully weighed against each other like the pairs of inscribed tablets placed in the pavilions,[6] and when one has thoroughly comprehended the tangible forms of objects one should endeavor to attain an inner communication with the soul of the garden and try to understand the mysterious forces governing the landscape and making it cohere."

The garden was for all seasons with their changing moods and colors, flowers and trees; so the pavilion and open gallery were necessary for enjoyment in the heat of summer or the cold of winter and became an integral part of the scenery. Even in winter one sat out in the pavilion to admire the beauties of the snow and to watch the budding of the almond and plum blossom. A portable brazier of glowing charcoal kept one warm and a large brazier was used to melt the snow to make tea. The garden was particularly evocative by

[6] Pairs of tablets were inscribed with parallel quotations which corresponded in tonal value and content.

Moon bridge and pavilion

Pavilion and rock

moonlight and the new and full moons, times of spiritual power, had their own festivals, especially the festival of the mid-autumn moon. Other festivals were also celebrated in the pavilion or garden; the vernal equinox, observed on the twelfth day of the second month of the Chinese year, was known as the Birthday of the Flowers.

Pavilions and galleries obviously had to blend with their surroundings. The *Yüan Yeh* says: "Buildings should be placed so as to harmonize with the natural formation of the ground." When pavilions were connected by galleries these followed the rise and fall and curves of the land or winding of the waters which were often crossed by bridges, bringing in all the symbolism of the crossing of the waters, of transition, of communication between one realm or plane and another as well as of man as mediator, occupying the central position between the great powers. Added beauty and symbolism was introduced in the "moon bridge", a lovely half-circle which when reflected in the clear water below formed the perfect circle of the full moon.

Roofs were curved and painted and the lattice work of the balustrades was lacquered and painted in harmonizing and symbolic colors. Harmony and proportion had to be maintained but symmetry was alien to Nature, thus the garden contained no such thing as clipped lawns or hedges or stiff geometrically designed flower beds, or flowers marshalled in rows or patterns. And "landscaping" had to absorb buildings and, like planted trees, make them look as if they had grown there. "One erects a pavilion where the view opens and plants flowers that smile in the face of the spring breeze."[7] It was a place for both relaxation and active enjoyment, for solitary meditation and study, or for convivial gatherings for friends to meet and drink tea or wine or take *al fresco* meals. There they composed poetry and music, painted, practiced calligraphy, or discussed philosophy. One amusement was to compose a poem in the time that it took a floating wine cup and saucer to drift from one end to the other on a meandering watercourse set in the floor of the pavilion. A poet failing to complete his poem in the time had to catch and empty the cup. These watercourses could also be constructed in symbolic forms such as the swastika, or the cross-form of the Chinese character for the number ten, or in the shape of a lotus or open flower. Sometimes the water tumbled over small waterfalls or rocks.

Pavilions were given names such as the Pavilion of the Hanging Rainbow, the Fragrance of the Lotus, the Secret Clouds, the Eight Harmonious Tones, Invitation or Contemplation of the Moon, Welcoming Spring, Pleasant Coolness and so on. In some gardens there were Halls of the Moon; these were constructed in the shape of a hemisphere, the vaulted ceiling painted to represent the nocturnal sky with innumerable small windows of colored glass depicting the moon and stars. The total effect was one of the subdued light of a summer's night. Sometimes the floor was planted with flowers, but more usually it contained running water, the moon and water being closely allied: "The moon washes its soul in the clear waters", but although moon and waters are both *yin*, water is symbolically related to the sun since the waters catch and reflect back the sun's light, the *yang*. These halls could be large enough for holding banquets or of a smallness suitable for intimate sitting about in conversation or listening to music and poetry. Here, in the garden, where heaven

[7] The *Yüan Yeh*.

The Mid-Lake Pavilion in the Lion Grove, Su-chou, Chiang-su province

and earth meet, music and poetry become the natural form of the expression of harmony.

While the pavilion was built in and for the garden and was open to it, this breaking down of the distinction between in and out of doors applied also to the dwelling house which was not only sited for *feng-shui* but for fitting as naturally as possible into the scenery and giving access so immediately to the garden that there seemed no dividing line. Doors either did not exist or were left open. (Socially, closed doors were not considered courteous since they implied exclusion, while the open door symbolized the welcome extended by the essentially out-going Chinese temperament with its spontaneous and natural relationships developed over the ages in the highly socialized life of a large family). Doors were often only a means of enhancing a view into the garden or to the scenery beyond, such as the moon door, a beautifully placed circle framing some special outlook. Not only was every aspect used to its full natural advantage but "if one can take advantage of a neighbor's view one should not cut off the communication, for such a 'borrowed prospect' is very acceptable".[8]

The house opened on to the garden and the garden came into the house; rooms opened on to the courtyards where flowering trees

[8] Ibid.

Pavilions and pond at Ching Hsin Hai, Pei Hai Park, Beijing

Courtyard in the North Temple Pagoda, Su-chou, Chiang-su province

Water-carved rocks in the Fisherman's Garden, Su-chou, Chiang-su province

grew and ferns and flowers fringed a central pool, usually with golden carp swimming in it, for the garden was a place for animal and bird life also. Indeed, animals and plants were not considered the only "living" things; everything shares in the cosmic power and mountains and rivers also "live". Nor was it at all unusual for the house to go out into the garden, for the lover of nature would move a bed out of doors, beside some special tree, shrub, or flower which was coming into bloom, so that no stage of its development and beauty would be lost; or one would sit up all night to enjoy the effect of the moonlight. "The moonlight lies like glittering water over the countryside. The wind sighs in the trees and gently touches the lute and the book that lie on the couch. The dark rippled mirror of the water swallows the half-moon. When day dawns one is awakened by the fresh breeze; it reaches the bed and all the dust of the world is blown out of one's mind."[9]

The garden was not, however, merely aesthetic but creative and a reminder of, and contact with, the creative forces and the great cycle of the seasons, birth, maturity, decay, death, and rebirth.

The merging of the native Taoism with imported Buddhism in Ch'an, or Zen, carried on the tradition of the intimate relationship between man and Nature. Ch'an Buddhism and gardens were two facets of Chinese inspiration which were adopted and carried on by the Japanese, but in later decadent times the original symbolism of the garden as a reflection of Paradise was lost and gardens became mere pleasure grounds, except where attached to monasteries in which much of the symbolism was taken over and where the association with meditation remained. In those gardens of effete times artificial extravagances crept in; windows were made in shapes which bore no relationship to symbols, such as teapots, animals, vases, and fans, even if some of these forms had, in fact, a symbolic content. But these aberrations were stigmatized by the *Yüan Yeh* as "stupid and vulgar" and "intelligent people should be careful in such matters".

The garden was a reflection of the macrocosm and embodied all the *yin-yang* dualisms projected in manifestation. Mountains, valleys, rivers, lakes, were all represented. As Cheng Pan ch'iao said: "The enjoyment of life should come from a view regarding the universe as a garden … so that all beings live according to their nature and great indeed is such happiness."

The importance of water in the Chinese garden was not only due to *yin-yang* symbolism but to the wide significance of water itself as, next to the Dragon, the greatest Taoist symbol. It is strength in weakness, fluidity, adaptability, coolness of judgment, gentle persuasion, and passionlessness. While mountains and rocks are the bones of the body and the earth its flesh, rivers and streams are the arteries and blood, life-giver and fertilizer. Flowing water and still water symbolized movement and repose and the complementary opposites, and water-worn stones represented the interaction of the soft and the hard. Still water also takes on all the symbolism of the mirror.

Water could be made by forming lakes and rivers in the earth excavated for making mountains, though mountains were most frequently represented by rocks, hollow and weather-worn, fretted out by the restless sea or the elements or formed from the strange shapes of petrified trees. These rocks were carefully selected for their color, texture, grain,

[9] Ibid.

and shape; some were upright and towering, others, larger at the top than at the base, gave the effect of disappearing into the clouds; others, lying down, took fantastic animal shapes, some gave out a note when struck, others were mute. Sometimes the rocks formed grottoes, but whatever the shape they always appeared as natural to the setting and were as near to the form of wild mountain crags as possible, giving the impression of Nature, untamed and capricious. (In this "naturalness" it must be remarked that the mountains of China in the Yangtze gorges, the far West, and the Southern provinces have been worked by nature herself into fantastic and sometimes grotesque shapes). "Try to make your mountains resemble real mountains. Follow Nature's plan" but "do not forget they have to be built by human hands".[10]

Symbolically, the mountain is, of course the world axis, but in the Chinese garden it also represented the *yang* power in Nature with the waters as the *yin*; the "mountain" is traditionally placed in the middle of a lake or pond, the rock being the stable and eternal, the water the flowing and temporal. This mountain-and-water (*shan shui*) symbolism also obtains in landscape painting. The rock and the shadow it casts are also *yang* and *yin*. Rocks are "silent, unmovable, and detached from life, like refined scholars". Their ruggedness also suggests the challenging and dangerous element in the mountains and in life.

In larger gardens the mountains were sufficiently high for the formation of small valleys and dales, with winding streams opening out into lakes on which boat journeys could be taken and where the water could be spanned by bridges. Sometimes a series of islands or rocks were so connected. Tunnels in the rocks gave the same effect and carried the same symbolism as bridges in passing from one world to another. But "even a little mountain may give rise to many effects ... a small stone may evoke many feelings".[11] Shen Fu says: "In the designing of a rockery or the training of flowering trees one should try to show the small in the large and the large in the small and provide for the real in the unreal and the unreal in the real. One reveals and conceals alternately, making it sometimes apparent and sometimes hidden."

Both the *yang* mountain and the *yin* tree are axial and so represent stability and balance between the two great powers; they also offer a line of communication for man between the celestial *yang* forces coming down to earth and the earthly *yin* forces reaching up to heaven, with man again as central and responsible for the maintenance of balance and harmony in responding equally to the *yin* and *yang* powers.

Trees were an essential feature of both the domestic and hermitage garden, particularly the latter where they were often the only addition made by man to the natural scenery and their variety was almost as important as the trees themselves. While all trees are beautiful and symbolize the feminine power, some were especially noted for their *yin-yang* qualities. Though *yin* as a tree, the pine and cedar express *yang* masculine dignity and rigidity in contrast to the feminine gracefulness, pliability, and charm of the willow, both these trees were considered necessary to maintain the *yin-yang* harmony. Flowering trees such as the almond, cherry, plum, and peach were esteemed—one should say loved—for their

[10] Ibid.

[11] Ibid.

Ma Yüan, *Apricot Blossoms*, Southern Sung dynasty

beauty and their symbolism. The almond, as the first flower of the year, is in many traditions the Awakener, watchfulness. As flowering in winter it is also courage in adversity. The cherry depicts delicacy of feeling and purity of feeling on the *yin* side and nobility on the *yang*. The plum, a symbol of winter and beauty signified strength and longevity and the hermit. It is one of the favorite subjects for artists and the plum, pine, and bamboo were called "the three friends of winter". The almond and plum are both symbolic of new life coming in spring, but the plum should have a gnarled trunk and branches, called sleeping dragons, as the *yang* to offset the delicate blossoms of the *yin*; they also represent the old and new together. Just as lovers of the garden would move their beds out under trees, so we read of artists who wandered all night in the moonlight to catch every phase of the beauty of "the dry limbs clad in jade-white blooms".

The peach holds a special position as the tree of the Taoist genii or Immortals; it is the Tree of Life at the center of Paradise. It is also the Tree of Immortality and one bite of the fruit growing on the tree in Paradise confers immediate immortality. Peach stones were apotropaic and were beautifully and symbolically carved and kept, or worn, as amulets and talismans. The tree is a symbol of spring, youth, marriage, wealth, and longevity.

Pre-eminent among flowers were the lotus, peony, and chrysanthemum. The peony is the only purely *yang* flower. Flowers, with their cup shape, naturally depict the *yin* receptive aspect in nature, but the peony is a royal flower, flaunting the red, fiery, masculine color; it is also nobility, glory, riches. The

Chrysanthemum and Rock, anonymous, Yüan dynasty, 14th century

chrysanthemum, on the other hand, is a flower of quiet retirement, the beloved flower of the cultured scholar, the retired official, who was of course also a scholar, and of the philosopher and poet. It was so much cultivated in retirement that it became a symbol of that life and of leisure. It signifies longevity as being that which survives the cold and as autumnal it is harvest and wealth, but it is primarily ease, leisure, joviality, and enjoyment. Yüan Chung-lang said that the retired and the scholar were fortunate in having "the enjoyment of the hills and water, flowers and bamboo" largely to themselves since "luckily they lie outside the scope of the strugglers for fame and power who are so busy with their engrossing pursuits that they have no time for such enjoyment".

But the lotus, a universal symbol in the East (its symbolism is taken on by the lily and sometimes the rose in the West) is "the flower that was in the Beginning, the glorious lily of the Great Waters ... that wherein existence comes to be and passes away". It is both *yin* and *yang* and contains within itself the balance of the two powers; it is solar as blooming in the sun and lunar as rising from the dark of the waters of pre-cosmic chaos. As the combination of air and water it symbolizes spirit and matter; its roots bedded in the darkness of the mud depict indissolubility; its stem, the umbilical cord of life, attaches man to his origins and is also a world axis; rising through the opaque waters of the manifest world, the leaves and flowers reach and unfold in the air and sunlight, typifying potentiality in the bud and spiritual expansion and realization in the flower; its seeds, moving on the waters are creation. The lotus is associated with the wheel both as the solar matrix and the sun-wheel of cycles of existence. Iamblicus calls it perfection, since its leaves, flowers, and fruit form the circle. As lunar-solar, *yin-yang*, the lotus is also the androgyne, the self-existent. It has an inexhaustible symbolism in Hinduism, Taoism, and Buddhism alike. Again it appears as both solar and lunar associated with sun gods such as Surya and lunar goddesses such as Lakshmi; solar with Amitabha and lunar with Kwan-yin and androgynous in Kwannon. The lotus is the Golden Flower of Taoism, the crystallization and experience of light, the Tao. While on the spiritual level it represents the whole of birth, growth, development, and potentiality, on the mundane level it depicts the scholar-gentleman who comes in contact with mud and dirty water but is uncontaminated by it. Apart from its almost endless symbolism, the lotus is a flower of great beauty and highly evocative; as Osvald Sirén says, a sheet of lotus blossom "emanates a peculiar magic, an atmosphere that intoxicates like fragrant incense and lulls like the rhythms of a rising and falling mantra".[12]

Ancient China understood many things which are only now reaching the West and being hailed as new discoveries. She anticipated by centuries the "discovery" that flowers and plants have feelings. Yüan Chung-lang knew that they have their likes and dislikes and compatabilities among other vegetation and that they respond to care and appreciation in more than a material way. The flowers in a Chinese garden were genuinely loved, not in any "precious" aestheticism, but rather in an intimate relationship between living individuals. He said that "flowers have their moods of happiness and sorrow and their time of sleep … when they seem drunk, or quiet and tired and when the day is misty, that is the sorrowful mood of flowers … when they bask in the sunlight and their delicate bodies are protected from the wind, that is the happy mood of flowers…. When the ancient people knew a flower was about to bud they would move their beds and pillows and sleep under it watching how the flower passed from infancy to maturity and finally dropped off and died…. As for all forms of noisy behavior and common vulgar prattle, they are an insult to the spirits of flowers. One should rather sit dumb like a fool than offend them."[13] Among things which flowers dislike are: too many guests; ugly women putting flowers in their hair; dogs fighting; writing poems by consulting a rhyming dictionary; books kept in bad condition; spurious paintings, and common monks talking Zen! On the other hand they do like a visiting monk who understands tea!

Picked flowers and vases of flowers should never be regarded as normal, only as a temporary expedient employed by those living in cities and unnatural places deprived of the hills and lakes or any garden.

For the town-dweller or for one kept indoors of necessity, the miniature garden was created. Though it was also seen in pavilions, it was most usually on the tables of scholars. It, too, symbolized Paradise, the Isles of the Blessed, or the Abode of the Immortals reflected in miniature perfection with the whole range of the *yin-yang* symbolism. Exceptionally beautiful stones or shells were used and there were miniature grottoes, trees, bamboos, and grasses growing among the mountains, valleys, and waters. The making of these gardens was an art in itself; just as Wang Wei maintained that the artist can bring all Nature into the space of a small painting, so the creator of a garden, large,

[12] *Gardens of China*.

[13] The treatise *P'ing Shih* by Yüan Chung-lang.

small, or miniature can concentrate the cosmos within its bounds.

Enclosing the whole garden in the city, or where the extent of the garden was limited, was the wall which was used not only as a boundary but as a setting for trees, shrubs, and flowers; it could also provide an aperture which opened up some special view. In the city, where space was restricted, walls were often a garden in themselves, sometimes built with considerable width with a roof-garden effect or with trees and shrubs planted on top and flowers and ferns in the crevices below. Enclosing walls also helped to make the city garden a place where one could find "stillness in turmoil". Apart from the symbolism of the enclosed garden the walls brought in the *yin-yang* significance of the interplay of light and shade.

Unfortunately, today China joins the industrial nations of the world in "exploiting" Nature. Hideous concrete blocks of flats, offices, and factories insulate man from any contact with the yellow earth and, sadly, Seyyed Hossein Nasr's words can be applied: "There is nearly total disequilibrium between modern man and nature as attested by nearly every expression of modern civilization which seeks to offer a challenge to nature rather than to co-operate with it.... The harmony between man and nature has been destroyed."[14] The *yin-yang* balance has been betrayed.

Lotus in Full Bloom, anonymous, Sung dynasty, 12th-13th century

[14] *Man and Nature*, Allen & Unwin, 1968.

12. TAOISM & HINDUISM

At the ancient capital of China at Ch'ang-an there existed a wide variety of religious faiths, with worship at their temples and shrines well established. Taoist and Confucianist temples represented the indigenous beliefs, while Buddhist shrines, Zoroastrian fire temples, Nestorian Christian churches, Islamic mosques, and Manichaean and Jewish groups continued peacefully side by side. Most died out as being alien to the Chinese temperament and mentality, but Buddhism, born of Hinduism, remained to become the third religion of China and was largely transformed into a distinctive Chinese Buddhism, and, fusing with Taoism, became Ch'an or Zen.

The comparison of Taoism with other religions is necessarily superficial in a small space, but it can provide an outline and indication for further interest. There are basic similarities in the perennial philosophy of all religions and, of necessity, they interact with one another, but similarities are not to be confused with identity; outwardly they are not one, they are many; it is the Power within them that is One. It is, naturally, in the mystic aspects of other religions that they have an affinity with Taoism and that in their dogmatic and theological forms that they part company.

Hinduism, like Taoism, lays stress on understanding rather than on action, so that ignorance becomes the opposite of the good and hence is the only real sin. The overcoming of ignorance is *avidya*, and ignorance as the source of all troubles is a common teaching in Hinduism, Taoism, and Buddhism. Self-knowledge, *moksha*, is the road to emancipation and the realization of the state of liberation from the illusions of the sense world. The doctrine of *maya*, or illusion, does not imply that this world is totally unreal but that it is a shadow-play, a reflection. It is the world of space and time, of extension and duration, of relativity, and is only real within its own boundaries; so also is evil in the world limited. *Maya*, although the doctrine does not appear specifically in Taoism, is reflected in manifestation in the in-breathing and out-breathing, creation and return, the evolution and involution of the *yin-yang*. It is only in the world of *maya* that duality exists: subject and object in Hinduism and Taoism are not ultimate entities but are involved in the play of forces in opposition which are to be overcome in the search for enlightenment and the final union of the self with the Self.

There is something reminiscent of the Taoist Hermit in the Hindu Forest Dweller: "I will take my lodging at the root of a tree, surrendering all things, loved as well as unloved, tasting neither grief nor pleasure, neither cherishing hope nor offering respect, free from the opposites, with neither fortune nor belongings." This, however, seems to lack the joy in nature characteristic of the Taoist attitude, although, on the other hand, for Hinduism the world is essentially an expression of delight, the play, *lila*, of the Absolute, which, however, is in no way bound by its creation.

Maya is basically the illusion which divides reactions and relationships into subject and object and gives rise to the pairs of opposites in the manifest world, seeing them as separate instead of totally interdependent. The word "illusion" is derived from the Latin to play a game, but play has its own rules, it is not haphazard, there are winning or losing choices and moves and throws which influence the outcome of the game and set an irrevocable force in motion. *Maya* is also that which can be measured and therefore involves limitation and finitude as opposed to the immeasurable and unbounded Absolute, *Atman*, or Tao. Yet another aspect of *maya* is that of a veil which can both conceal and reveal. It is illusory simply because it is a partial view and partial truth: only the whole truth is illuminating. The viewpoint alters with the level of perception and awareness, as, for example in the classic case of the snake and the coil of rope; the amount of light available for seeing and the ability to observe accurately can completely change the thing seen. Any viewing from outside is liable to distortion. The lower levels are certainly contained in the higher, but it is only from the higher level that it can be appreciated that the other levels are lower, partial truths. They still partake of the nature of truth, but only in a fragmentary manner. The level of manifestation is a limitation in the realm of becoming which is ultimately transcended to reach the level of Being and Truth.

Maya is a reflected world. It is illusory in that the reflection can never be the thing-in-itself, but it is real in that the reflections can shadow forth the presence of the Real and, once known for what it is, can be the means of leading to the Real. In this reflected world things merely appear distinct and discrete because they are caught up in the time-space continuum and seem to follow each other; the coming into being and passing from it are illusions of time. This succession of changes is perceived by mind and created by mind.

One branch of Indian idealism speaks of "perfuming", just as the clothes we wear have no personal scent of their own but take on a distinctive aroma when worn. The real "suchness" or "that which is" is the original thing-in-itself which is untainted by "perfuming", which comes from ignorance and is the power of illusion in the world. "That which is" is pure, that which is manifest is tainted by duality and becomes an illusion of the ego and of separateness. Once the ignorance and illusion are recognized the "perfuming" power works in reverse and leads to an understanding of the truth and releasing from the bonds of illusion, leading the individual to the *dharma* and the way back to the Real.

Awareness, *cit*, is the Essence which makes possible the transcendence of the realm of illusion of the senses in the phenomenal world. The system of Patanjali aims more at the control of the mind than at union with the ultimate and appears to accept a fundamental dualism not present in Taoism. The dualism of *purusha* and *prakriti*, subject and object is absolute in Samkhya, the yoga of Patanjali, each having its own eternal existence, as opposed to the non-dualistic school of *Vedanta* which is committed to belief in the Absolute, a Supreme Being with which union is possible. The God of *Advaita-Vedanta* is the efficient cause of the Universe; from *Brahman* issues the whole cosmos: in manifestation "It" is Isvara, or any other divine name.

Hinduism is rightly and naturally polytheistic in the world of manifestation, but monotheistic in the doctrine of the One, *Brahman*. Apparent polytheism is, in fact, a unified plurality, or the action in multiplic-

Chao Meng-fu (1254-1322), *The Mind Landscape of Hsieh Yuyü*, Yüan dynasty

ity of the One. A pantheon also appeared in late Taoism, borrowed largely from Buddhism which had carried over much from Hinduism.

In the *Upanishads*, *Brahman* and *Atman* are names expressing the Primordial Principle, or Tao; they do not imply a deity to be worshipped in any personal sense, but express that which is beyond all forms and phenomena but from which all has arisen. In It all dualities are resolved. It may be fully equated with the Tao as impersonal Spirit, the Supreme Power of the universe, beyond the reach of the senses and the rational mind; It is the unqualified and limitless. "*Brahman* has neither name nor form, transcends merit and demerit, it is beyond time, space, and the objects of sense-experience. Such is *Brahman*, and thou art That." "Supreme, beyond the power of speech to express, *Brahman* may yet be apprehended by the eye of pure illumination. Pure, absolute, and eternal Reality." Of *Atman* it is said: "Grasping without hands, hastening without feet, it sees without eyes, it hears without ears. It knows what is to be known, but no one knows it."[1] "From it the universe comes forth, into it the universe merges, and in it the universe breathes."[2] Taoism parallels this with: "When the Ten Thousand Things are viewed in their oneness, we return to the Origin and remain where we have always been."[3] And there is no better definition of the Tao than Krishna's saying: "I, oh Arjuna, am that which is and that which is not."[4]

[1] *Shvetashvatara Upanishad.*

[2] *Chhandogya Upanishad.*

[3] Sen T'sen. Third Patriarch of the Ch'an School of Buddhism.

[4] *Bhagavad Gita*, IX.

Chung-li Ch'üan Seeking the Tao, Ming dynasty, 15th century

What for Sri Ramana Maharshi is the Self, is in every respect applicable to the Tao. The Self cannot be "attained" since, like the Tao, it is all and contains all; it must be realized, but even then that expression involves the implication of separation. It is rather a case of "be what thou art" or in the Maharshi's own words: "If the Self were to be reached it would mean that the Self is not now and here, but that it should be got anew. What can be got afresh can also be lost. So it will be impermanent. What is not permanent is not worth striving for. So I say the Self is not reached. You are the Self. You are already That." Although Taoism does not actually speak of the inner Self as the Tao, it may be fair to say that since "beyond the Self there is nothing",[5] it may be equated with the Tao.

The *Upanishad*s speak of One Being which divided itself into Two, the male and female, and brought about the existence of the cosmos. Radha and Krishna each derive power from the interplay and interaction with the other. (Indian symbolism is here expressed in more physical terms than those used in the more abstract Chinese mode.) This is also the symbolism of Shiva and his *shakti* in the upward and downward pointing triangles, representing fire and the male, with water and the female element. These have their counterparts in *purusha*, mind, male, and *prakriti*, matter, female, Essence and Substance. Every Indian deity is balanced by his consort and this *yin-yang* symbolism is evidenced in Hinduism in the representation of the androgynous Shiva and Parvati, which involves the full significance of the opposites and complementaries, but is expressed in a more sexual form than the *yin-yang*. Balance is also stressed in the Hindu theory of the qualities of Nature, the two opposites of the active and the inert, the

[5] *Katha Upanishad.*

rajas and *tamas*, with *sattva*, balance, as the resolving third. A passage from the *Bhagavad Gita*[6] also echoes the Taoist actionless-action of *wu-wei*: "The action that is obligatory is done without love or hate by one who desires no fruit and who is free from attachment—that action is characterized by *sattva*, balance."

The *Gita* teaches that it is not necessary to renounce the world. There should be no real conflict between ordinary and spiritual life; all that is necessary is to act without attachment. "Not by abstention from action does a man enjoy actionlessness".[7] This detachment in both Hinduism and Buddhism is the same as the acceptance of Taoism since in each case there is no rejection of the occurrences of daily life, coupled with an acceptance of all experience with an evenness and openness of mind. As Krishna says to Arjuna: "Neither let your motive be the fruit of action, nor let your attachment be to non-action.... Perform your actions casting off attachment and remaining even-minded in success and failure." "He who sees inaction in action and action in inaction—he is wise among men, he is a *yogi*, he has performed all action."

The *yogi*, whose aim is union with the Real, the Absolute of non-dualistic Vedanta, recognizes the importance of the body as an instrument for the development of the spiritual and so works for a perfect physical and mental balance which will lead to supra-physical and supra-mental states of awareness. As a preliminary to this realization he must resolve the dualistic conflicts so that he is no longer caught up in the unrealities of *maya*. Rhythm in the physical and mental functions is, as in later Taoism, obtained by breathing and other exercises. Some branches of yoga tended towards asceticism, austerities, and world-renunciation, and in Taoism this alien factor crept in with the "Hygiene School", which attempted to develop the ability to do without food through breathing techniques—literally living on air! This was a radical departure from classical Taoism and yoga, with its "letting-go" of *wu-wei*, and the natural release from all that is restricting and artificial. There is a vast difference between the controlled practices of yoga in reducing the demands of the sensual and instinctive life and so rendering the body a fit vehicle for the journey towards enlightenment, and a self-torturing of the body which renders the body weak and useless. The yoga of later, decadent Taoism had lost the earlier spiritual aims embodied in Hindu yoga and was directed towards the pursuit of personal immortality through transmutation of the gross body into a subtle body capable of surviving apparent death. The real aim of yoga was ignored or lost, that of union with the One, or the Tao, of metaphysical Taoism. Alchemical Taoism, with its cult of the immortality of the body, had certain affinities with *hatha-yoga* in this bodily cult and in its name which is solar-lunar and so approximates the *yin-yang* or *Shiva-shakti* polarity. There seems to be some confusion as to what was meant by this immortality. In some cases it was undoubtedly a striving for perfect physical health and attempting to find the means of bodily immortality; in other ways it appears more in the nature of an alchemical transformation which, through yoga, formed a higher, non-material, immortal body.

Original Taoism had nothing in common with *bhakti-yoga*, the way of devotion to a personal God, coupled with sacrifice, except in its final aim of union. The intellectual *jnana-yoga* and the contemplative *raja-yoga* were more

[6] Ch. XVIII.
[7] III. 4.

Magical Palaces of the Immortals, silk tapestry, anonymous, Sung dynasty

in accord with traditional Taoism, but *jnana-yoga*, though the way of knowledge and intuition, discrimination and discernment, parts company with Taoism when it teaches renunciation and austerity; not that its austerities were the masochism of the ascetic. *Karma-yoga* has an affinity with the actionless-action of Taoism. Action is an essential part of life, but this action is unattached, unmotivated: "Therefore, without attachment perform always the work that has to be done, for man attains to the highest by doing work without attachment."[8]

The *Yogasikha Upanishad* teaches that neither yoga nor knowledge by themselves lead to emancipation, but both should be practiced. But meditation and yogic exercises practiced merely for the relief of the tremendous tensions of modern life but divorced from their spiritual background, are ultimately more dangerous than helpful since they give temporary relief which imparts a false sense of security but fail to deal with the root of the trouble, spiritual malaise, merely enabling people to live with their illusions instead of curing them.

[8] *Bhagavad Gita*, III.19.

13. TAOISM & BUDDHISM

Buddhist priests were said to have arrived in China, from India, at the Chinese capital in the reign of Ch'in Shih-huang-ti, between 221 and 208 B.C. It was said that there were Buddhist monks at Ch'ang-an in the second half of the second century B.C., but these assertions cannot be verified definitely. Traders traveled along the Silk Route and entered North West China at Tun-huang and both they and the Buddhist monks settled in the towns. Later, Chu shih-hsing journeyed to Khotan, in the middle of the third century B.C. to obtain Buddhist scriptures and brought back the Sanskrit *Prajna-paramita*, which greatly influenced Chinese Buddhist thought, while Fa Hu (c. 266-308) translated the Mahayanist *Lotus of the True Doctrine* and in A.D. 399 Fa-hsien left Ch'ang-an on a pilgrimage to India to study sacred texts and to persuade Indian Buddhist teachers to go to China.

The T'ang dynasty saw an increase of pilgrims to India. Hsuan-tsang (c. 596-664) left China in 629 and did not arrive back until 645, having studied at Nalanda University. He brought back Sutras and relics in quantity and thereafter did an enormous amount of translation work. In 677 I-sing took the sea route to India from Canton and he both translated and wrote Buddhist works. From Nalanda, Padmasambhava traveled to convert Tibet to Buddhism in the eighth century, developing the distinctive form of Tibetan Buddhism.

Both Sanskrit and classical Chinese were languages of a literary elite and were not available to anyone other than the scholar, so that original Buddhism in China was an intellectual philosophy and found itself closely akin to metaphysical Taoism but had little in common with classical Confucianism, which was based on ethics and regarded the family as a sacred institution and filial piety as a sacred duty; indeed Buddhism actually conflicted with the Confucian ideal in discouraging family life and encouraging celebacy. Also the rigidity of the rules controlling the life of the Confucian scholar was unacceptable to Taoism and Buddhism, both of which laid stress on fluidity and adaptability.

In propagating their religion the early Buddhist missionaries, and their Chinese converts, made considerable use of Taoist philosophy and phraseology in translating the Sutras and in demonstrating the compatibility of the Buddhist faith with the indigenous Taoist culture. For example, in early Buddhism *wu-wei* was used to express Nirvana, as actionless-action, the cessation of dualistic activity; also the Way of Tao was equated with the Path leading to Nirvana, and Buddha was described as "the one who does nothing yet there is nothing he does not do". As early Buddhism borrowed from Taoism, so later Taoism borrowed from the pantheon which developed in Buddhism until the two became almost indistinguishable and both popular Taoism and Buddhism shared and were dominated by the ubiquitous spirits, good and bad, which had constantly to be consulted and propitiated.

Buddhism and Taoism are in accord

Confucius presenting the young Gautama Buddha to Lao Tzu, Ch'ing dynasty

nearly all the way, only diverging in a small, though vital, point: that of the attitude to life's vicissitudes. Buddhism has been accused of pessimism, not altogether fairly, but it does adopt an attitude to life in this world which sees it as suffering, as the result of desire, and as something from which to escape. Taoism, on the other hand, teaches the acceptance of things as they are and views life as something basically good and to be enjoyed, having here an affinity with the Parsee belief in "the good life". Taoism also has a more humorous approach to life. Chuang Tzu's book abounds in humor, sometimes mocking and mordant, but laughter is never far off. However, in Buddhism we have Buddhaghosa speaking of the cheerfulness of the *arhat*, or Sage, "who is distinguished by and noted for his cheerful temperament",[1] and the Ch'an Master Tao-shin said: "It is all joy, free from anxiety—it is called Buddha." The Buddhist teaching on suffering does not imply that all life is misery, but that sorrow and suffering are inevitable in human existence and its aim is to free mankind from that state by going beyond it to enlightenment; the chief means of so doing being to dispel ignorance and see things as they are. Nor does Buddhism encourage the self-inflicted suffering of asceticism: "By suffering, the emaciated devotee produces confusion and sickly thoughts in his mind. Mortification is not conducive even to worldly knowledge, how much less to a triumph over the senses."[2] Both Taoism and Buddhism insist on a total living in the present moment, not clinging to or regretting a dead past, nor meeting or speculating on a future before it arrives, but seeing into the present nature of things. There is an Indian saying that you cannot ride the camel that has gone, nor mount the camel that is not yet here. Moment-to-moment living solves problems as they arise, gives a clearer, more direct view of their content, and prevents anxiety and worry which always involve a merely hypothetical future which may never come.

Both religions are non-theistic, maintaining that "God", or the Tao, or Nirvana are beyond conceptual thought; they discourage speculation and "discursive thought". Buddha said: "By allaying the initial and discursive thought, with the mind inwardly tranquillized and fixed on one point, I entered into and abided in the second *jnana* which is devoid of initial and discursive thought.... I dwelt with even-mindedness, mindful and clearly conscious."

Reason with its clear-cut either/or, right or wrong, fact or fiction, is limited to the manifest world and cannot go beyond it; it has its uses in the realm of duality, but exceeds its legitimate function when it tries to concern itself with the infinite or the ultimate, also, being in duality it must always give rise to conflict and argument and so often it depends on facts which are selected to fit the theories: "the jungle of theorizing, the wilderness of theorizing, the tangle of theorizing, the bondage and shackles of theorizing, attended by ill, distress, perturbation, and fever; it conduces not to detachment, passionlessness, tranquility, peace, to knowledge and wisdom of Nirvana."[3] Nirvana and the Tao are both the ultimate resolution of all opposites where there is "neither this world nor any other world, neither sun nor moon",[4] yet "the life of the world is the same as Nirvana and really there is no difference between them at all".[5] "Only those whose minds no longer measure things understand Nirvana which they grasp not nor reject ... for them the three times and both extremes have disappeared."[6] The Ch'an Master answering the question "What is Tao?" replied: "Ordinary life is the very Tao"; and "What is Tao?",—"Eat when you are hungry and sleep when you are tired."

Taoism and Ch'an, later Zen in Japan, use the same language; the Self-Nature of Buddhism and the Tao are one and the same. The Sixth Patriarch was told that Ch'an Masters at the capital were teaching that "if one wishes

[1] *Visuddhimagga*, XV. 43.

[2] *The Sermon at Benares*.

[3] *Majjhima-Nikaya*.

[4] *Udana*, 80.

[5] *Nagarjuna Madhyamika Karika*, XXV.

[6] *Altar Sutra* of the Sixth Patriarch.

Three Laughing Men by the Tiger Stream, a painting depicting a Confucian priest, a Taoist official, and a Buddhist monk, Sung dynasty, c. 1296

to understand Tao one should sit in *dhyana* meditation and practise *samadhi*", but the Patriarch replied: "Tao is to be understood by the awakening mind and has nothing to do with sitting in meditation.... The Tathagata has neither whence to come nor whither to go, because it is beyond birth and death."[7]

Ch'an was the synthesis of Taoism and Buddhism. The Buddhist Patriarch Bodhidharma, the "Bearded Barbarian", as the Chinese called him, arrived in China from India at the golden age of Chinese culture. In meeting Taoism the two philosophies had so much in common that it was not surprising that a fusion took place and produced the Ch'an school. It, as with original Taoism and Buddhism, arose as a protest against the development of formalism and speculation and advocated a return to simplicity. Both recognized two methods of attaining enlightenment, gradual progression, or sudden illumination. The sudden or "abrupt" way aims at shocking the disciple into an immediacy of experience, as Gai Eaton puts it: "To cut, with a well-aimed thrust, through the curtain which shuts out the light". Here, the rational mind is a hindrance and source of delusions and limitations; it functions in the realm of the senses, indeed, in Eastern religions it is the sixth sense. We are not simple-minded enough and allow both mind and emotions to interfere with direct perception; this is the Taoist-Buddhist doctrine of No-mind.

Taoist and Ch'an masters are indistinguishable and are represented as wizened men laughing in the face of self-righteousness and worldly values of such things as fame and fortune, taking neither themselves nor anyone else too seriously. Theirs is the effortless-effort, actionless-action, coupled with an inherent lightness of touch and lightness of spirit. Weight is of the earth, lightness is a

[7] *Altar Sutra.*

quality of the spirit. Though remaining impersonal and detached, the personal and immediate are enjoyed in the everyday world in a total freedom from attachment

Possibly the most significant concept passed on by Taoism into Ch'an is that of immediacy and spontaneity necessary for living in accord with Nature and for simplicity, motiveless action, and the perfection of effortlessness. When Ch'an reached Japan and became known as Zen, this spontaneity influenced all branches of Japanese art, in painting, poetry, archery, and fencing, all demanding instantaneous response which gives the thinking mind no time to interfere; no deliberation, no alteration is possible, and, as in Taoism, with simplicity and spontaneity come joy, lightheartedness, and the totally carefree spirit; of this freedom Hui Neng, the Ch'an Patriarch said: "The only difference between a Buddha and an ordinary man is that one realizes it and the other does not". This freedom is also the Taoist *wu-wei*, letting-go, non-assertion, moving with the currents of life and Nature and so avoiding friction and allowing the upsurge of the natural rhythms of life, both physical and spiritual. "Use the light within you to revert to your natural clearness of sight. No need to look for it outside."[8]

Hinayana Buddhism has less affinity with Taoism than has the Mahayana; the former, with its stress on the control of the body and its strong dualism, has more in common with later, popular Taoism which developed its own forms of yogic practices, as in alchemical Taoism and the "Hygiene School" which taught breath control, fasting, hygiene, and cultivation of the body, as did *hatha-yoga*; its devotees were vegetarian, abstained from wine, and were celebate, their aim being first longevity in a healthy physical and mental state in this life, then a happy survival in the Western Paradise. Earlier Taoism and Mahayana aimed at the development of wisdom in the making of the Sage or Enlightened One and the attaining of the Tao or Nirvana. The Pure Land Buddhism and later Taoism both promulgated the idea of the Western

Ting Yun-p'eng (1584-1638), *Masters of the Three Religions*, Ming dynasty

[8] *Altar Sutra.*

Portrait of the Six Dynasties Taoist Master T'ao Hungching (451-536), Yüan dynasty, 14th century

Paradise, to which souls of the virtuous and fortunate gained entrance at death, and early Chinese Buddhism is shown as teaching the existence of an immortal soul; Yüan Hung, of the Han dynasty, wrote in his *Hou Han Chi*, that Buddhists "also teach that when a man dies his soul does not perish but will be reborn and take another form". And Hui yüan wrote: "While the body dissolves, the spirit does not change. With the unchanging spirit availing itself of the changing body, there is no end to the transformations."[9] But these teachings were a departure from the original precepts of their founders, since the concept of the Western Paradise conflicted with the non-personal nature of the Tao and the Buddhist Nirvana. Both the Buddhist *Sunyata* and the Taoist Void, Emptiness or Ultimate Reality, are inner, not outward, states and beyond definition. Of *Sunyata* it is written: "Nothing comes into existence, nor does anything disappear. Nothing is eternal, nor does it have an end." Of the Tao it is said, "It is the formless yet complete", it "stands alone and never changes, it pervades everywhere and is never exhausted".[10]

Tantric Buddhism, which became specifically the form of Buddhism in Tibet, rose from yogic practices but transcended them. It is an interpretation of a relative dualism such as exists in Hinduism in the symbolism of *Shiva-shakti*, and the union of male and female which appears in a more humanized version of the more abstract *yin-yang* symbol, the union of the two resulting in the merging of their dual identities into the androgyne, the non-dualistic One. This Tantric union is analogous with the marriage of Wisdom and Method, *prajna* and *upaya*, *yin* and *yang*, though Tantric Buddhism does not fully equate the feminine principle with *shakti* so much as with *prajna*, Wisdom, and although employing the female-male polarity, it, like Taoism in the *yin-yang*, implies no sexuality in the symbolism. The one is transcendent and aloof, the other immanent and playing a part in the world. The *yin-yang* symbolism also appears in the concept of the body being composed of two elements, the diamond element, the male, active, material, and the womb element, the female, passive and mental.

S. B. Dasgupta writes of Tantra as: "a theological principle of duality in non-duality.... The ultimate non-dual Reality possesses two aspects in its fundamental nature, the negative (*nivritti*) and the positive (*pravritti*), the static and dynamic.... These two aspects are represented in Hinduism by Shiva and Shakti and in Buddhism by *prajna* and *upaya*, or *Sunyata* and *karuna*."[11]

In Tantrism the senses, which are normally an agent binding man to the body, are used as a means of release from their tyranny and as an aid to the understanding of the relationship of the body to the spirit and the spirit to the divine.

Tantrism and Taoism, however, part company in their practical application for while traditional Taoism was ritual-free, spontaneous, and unconventional, Tantrism is highly ritualistic, though one school did maintain that ritual was a hindrance and enlightenment was attained by the sudden stroke or spontaneous illumination.

[9] *Shen-pu-mieh-lun*. On the Indestructability of the Soul.

[10] *Tao Te Ching*, XXV.

[11] *An Introduction to Tantric Buddhism.*

ILLUSTRATIONS

INDEX

For a glossary of all key foreign words used in books published by World Wisdom, including metaphysical terms in English, consult:
www.DictionaryofSpiritualTerms.org.
This on-line Dictionary of Spiritual Terms provides extensive definitions, examples and related terms in other languages.

BIOGRAPHICAL NOTES

JEAN C. COOPER was born in 1905 at Chefoo in North China. She was brought up by Chinese amahs (nurses) to understand Taoism, Confucianism, and Buddhism, the three religions of China. She went to a British school at Kuling in the mountains of Lushan, traveled the world with her parents, and finished her education at boarding school in England. Cooper read Philosophy at St. Andrew's University and lectured on Comparative Religion, Philosophy, and Symbolism, chiefly in adult education. She lived with her husband in an ideal state of rural seclusion and beauty in the county of Cumberland in the North-West of England (the Wordsworth country). The Taoists say that one should have a simple dwelling, facing south, with running water by it and woods behind it. She had just that.

Cooper is the author of numerous works, including *Taoism: The Way of the Mystic*, *Yin & Yang: The Taoist Harmony of Opposites*, *Chinese Alchemy: The Taoist Quest for Immortality*, *Brewer's Book of Myth and Legend*, *Symbolism: The Universal Language*, *An Illustrated Encyclopedia of Traditional Symbols*, *Cassell Dictionary of Christianity*, and *Fairy Tales: Allegories of the Inner Life*. She was an untiring reader of books on spirituality and comparative religion, and contributed many book reviews to the journal *Studies in Comparative Religion*. She died in 1999.

WILLIAM STODDART was born in Carstairs, Scotland, lived most of his life in London, England, and now lives in Windsor, Ontario. He studied modern languages, and later medicine, at the universities of Glasgow, Edinburgh, and Dublin. For many years Stoddart was assistant editor of the British journal *Studies in Comparative Religion*. Pursuing his interests in comparative religion, he has traveled widely in Europe, North Africa, India, Ceylon, and Japan. Stoddart's works include *Sufism: The Mystical Doctrines and Methods of Islam*, *Outline of Hinduism*, *Outline of Buddhism*, *Invincible Wisdom: Quotations from the Scriptures, Saints, and Sages of All Times and Places*, and *What Do the Religions Say About Each Other?* His essential writings were published by World Wisdom as *Remembering in a World of Forgetting: Thoughts on Tradition and Postmodernism*.

JOSEPH A. FITZGERALD is an award-winning editor whose previous publications include *Honen the Buddhist Saint: Essential Writings and Official Biography*, *The Way and the Mountain: Tibet, Buddhism, and Tradition*, *The Essential Sri Anandamayi Ma: Life and Teachings of a 20th Century Indian Saint*, *Of the Land and the Spirit: The Essential Lord Northbourne on Ecology and Religion* (with Christopher James), *A Christian Woman's Secret: A Modern-Day Journey to God*, and *The Cheyenne Indians: Their History and Lifeways*. For more than twenty years he has traveled extensively to traditional cultures throughout the world, including South Asia and India. He studied Comparative Religion at Indiana University, where he also earned a Doctor of Jurisprudence degree, and lives with his wife and daughters in Bloomington, Indiana.

Titles in the Treasures of the World's Religions series by World Wisdom

The Essential Vedānta: A New Source Book of Advaita Vedānta, edited by Eliot Deutsch and Rohit Dalvi, 2004

For God's Greater Glory: Gems of Jesuit Spirituality, edited by Jean-Pierre Lafouge, 2006

The Golden Chain: An Anthology of Pythagorean and Platonic Philosophy, selected and edited by Algis Uždavinys, 2004

The Heart of Plotinus: The Essential Enneads, edited by Algis Uždavinys, 2009

An Illustrated Introduction to Taoism: The Wisdom of the Sages, by Jean C. Cooper, edited by Joseph A. Fitzgerald, 2010

In the Heart of the Desert, Revised: The Spirituality of the Desert Fathers and Mothers, by John Chryssavgis, 2008

Native Spirit: The Sun Dance Way, by Thomas Yellowtail, 2007

Native Spirit and The Sun Dance Way, as told by Thomas Yellowtail, documentary DVD, directed by Jennifer Casey, 2007

Not of This World: A Treasury of Christian Mysticism, compiled and edited by James S. Cutsinger, 2003

Pray Without Ceasing: The Way of the Invocation in World Religions, edited by Patrick Laude, 2006

Zen Buddhism: A History, Vol. I: India and China, by Heinrich Dumoulin, 2005

Zen Buddhism: A History, Vol. II: Japan, by Heinrich Dumoulin, 2005